GW00836655

MIKE
BREWER
THE AUTHORISED BIOGRAPHY

MIKE
BREWER
THE AUTHORISED BIOGRAPHY

WITH PHIL GIFFORD

nP books **rugby publishing limited**
Auckland, New Zealand

© 1995 Phil Gifford, Mike Brewer
First published in 1995 by Rugby Publishing Ltd,
67-73 View Road, Glenfield, Auckland 10, New Zealand.

Layout/design by Sportz Graphics Ltd, Takapuna, Auckland.
Typeset by Sports Graphics Ltd.
Printed by Griffin Paperbacks, Netley, South Australia.

Rugby Publishing Ltd is a member of the Medialine Group of Companies.
P.O. Box 100-243 North Shore Mail Centre, Auckland 10, New Zealand.

ISBN 0-908630-53-0

All rights reserved. No part of the publication may be reproduced or transmitted
in any form or by any means electronic or mechanical, including photocopy,
recording or any information retrieval system, without permission in writing
from the publisher.

CONTENTS

DEDICATED TO BEV AND HARRISON

1

The Age of Innocence

T he ego-free climb is a great time to be in a team. A group comes together, with no great record of past success, and puts aside selfishness, and individual competitiveness to benefit the team.

In my career I've been lucky enough to be involved in several ego-free climbs, with Otago, Canterbury, and the All Blacks. All share common ground; a unity of purpose, strong leadership, and almost inevitable success. And the ego-free climb almost demands innocence. Cynicism can wreck a business, and it can wreck a team.

If you asked most New Zealand rugby fans to name an All Black side that springs to mind when you mention the word innocent, most would surely think of the 1986 All Blacks who played France, the Baby Blacks.

Some of the players in that side have said they didn't like the Baby Blacks term, but really, if we were perceived as a bunch of kids taking on a man-sized job, that wasn't far from the reality.

Remember the circumstances: The 30 players the All Black selectors had considered the best in the country the previous year had been denied a trip to South Africa because of private legal action. In '86 they toured Africa as an unofficial team, called the Cavaliers, coached by a New Zealand rugby legend, Colin Meads, the famous Pinetree.

The New Zealand Rugby Union announced that all the Cavaliers would be banned from the first two tests of the home season, a one off game with France, and the first of a three test series against Australia. Pinetree's men had opened the door for 15 hopefuls to wear the All Black jersey.

The first dealings I had with Colin Meads, and my first taste of rugby at a national level, involved a crisis over a haircut.

In 1985 I was selected for the New Zealand Colts team, who had an internal tour, then had to face the Australian Colts at Eden Park. I was appointed captain, and was lucky enough to have Pinetree as coach, and JJ Stewart, the former All Black coach, as manager.

When we arrived in Wanganui for the first game Grant Mickell, the big Canterbury loose forward, went and had a haircut. It was the $40 special, and he got his money's worth. They left a little pigtail at the back, and that was bleached. The sides were short, but they were dyed pink.

Grant, and the haircut, were going up the stairs of the hotel as Pinetree was going down. The Tree just stared, then he came straight to my room.

"Have you seen that bloody Mickell?"

"No, I haven't. Why?"

"He's got the worst f***in' haircut I've ever seen in my life. Now this is your job. You tell him that if it's not fixed by 2 o'clock he's going home."

Poor old Grant. It cost him $40 to upset Pinetree, and I don't know what it cost when he raced back to get the pigtail off, and the dye taken out.

Actually Pinetree was a good man to have in charge of a bunch of 21-year-olds. While he wasn't that open minded about hairstyles, he was easy to talk to, and he had a basic, but I believe very sound, philosophy about training. You trained harder than you have to play.

In Pinetree's view if you find out what pain and hurt is while you're training, then when you face it in a game you know what it is to go through it. Before training proper began he insisted that everyone in the team run four laps round the outside of the field. Players now might say it was monotonous, and there was no need to do it, but I think it's a good idea. You did it in your own time, not as a group, and then you kicked a ball, or whatever you wanted to do, until everyone was finished. It was good for getting soreness out, and the blood pumping. And it was part of the disciplined culture he bred into the team in a very short time.

We were a side with a lot of talented players. Greg Cooper, Bernie McCahill, John Schuster, Marty Berry and Zinzan Brooke would all become All Blacks and several more like Alan Crowley, Phil Coffin, Greg Coffey, Brett Iti and Jim Coe would have long provincial careers. The selectors did make one obvious blunder. In the trial the Possibles flanker Michael Jones scored two tries, but missed out on the team.

JJ Stewart and Pinetree bounced off each other well. JJ has a keen sense of humour, which he showed early in the tour when Zinny and Bernie McCahill made a call that we all had to wear pink socks with our number ones (the black blazer, shirt and tie outfit). We had a meeting and Pinetree crossed his legs. We couldn't believe it…he was wearing pink socks.

There were a few sniggers, and then JJ took the floor.

"It is important, if we're to succeed as a team, for everyone to be thinking along the same lines. That's why everyone must wear the uniform properly, and to be dressed exactly the same way.

"Having said that, I have to tell you this. There is no way in the world that I'm prepared to wear pink socks." He hitched up his trousers a bit, and we could see he was wearing black dress shoes, with no socks at all.

JJ found it easy to relate to, and communicate with, young players. And a lot of what he said was extremely relevant. How you could only keep being successful if the desire you began with was still there. How you should avoid panic on the field, but learn to absorb the feel of how the game was evolving. How important correct decision making was. How vital it was to get over the advantage line and put pressure on your opponents.

In the second game, against Manawatu, we found out what pressure meant. They had a very strong pack then, with All Blacks Gary Knight and Geoff Old two of the strongmen. We were ahead

11

9-6 at halftime, and we'd had the wind. It was a really physical game, and we took the option of running the blind all through the second half. Our halfback, Alan Crowley, did it superbly, and we finally beat them, 15-9.

On the Wednesday we got to Auckland, with our "test" against the Australians on the Saturday. We expected a nice easy run. Instead, Pinetree ran us into the ground. With the intensity of the games, his preparation on and off the field, and JJ's advice and help, we were able to give the Australians a good hiding, 37-21. We scored four tries, while all their points came from kicks.

The whole Colts tour was a great learning experience for me. In less than 12 months the banning of the Cavaliers threw it wide open for a bunch of us who had not even played a lot of first division rugby.

There were going to be two trials in '86, so if you could string two good games together, you were in with a royal show. All of us who were candidates had grown up in an era when rugby was even bigger than it is now as a national sport. You could feel the urgency, how hard guys were striving to be in the team.

At the first trial, in Blenheim, I was in what was supposed to be the shadow test pack, and we had a good game, really blowing the Probables off the field. Peter Fatialofa had a very good game that day, and I thought he might have snuck into the side. Then we moved to Oamaru for a North Island-South Island game. By now it seemed to be down to either myself or the Auckland No 8, John McDermott, for the back row position. Mark Brooke-Cowden, from Auckland, and Andy Earl, from Canterbury, seemed to have the siderow spots sewn up. The North won the inter-island game, 22-10, but when the All Black team was announced, I was in at No 8.

Then, for the first time in what was a short rugby career, just over one season in the first division, self doubt really got to me.

I started to think, "Am I really good enough to pull on this jersey, and represent New Zealand after all the great No 8s who have gone before me?" The one thing I didn't want to do was to play the game and not measure up. There were a lot of times when I lay awake at night, the stomach churning. The thought was always the same: "What'll happen if I have a shocker? I'll never play for New Zealand again."

That unease carried right through until the captain's meeting the night before the game. When we assembled at the old Avon Hotel on Oxford Terrace in Christchurch most of us had to introduce ourselves to each other. I'd never met Andy Earl before. To be brutally honest, I'd never even heard of Brent Harvey, the Wairarapa-Bush flanker, before the trials. There's never been anything like it in my experience.

We were basically a group of strangers, and at first we trained like it. Brian Lochore, the coach, ran us very hard on the Thursday at the Burnham Army camp. It was so physical at scrum time that Bruce Hemara, the Manawatu hooker, popped a rib, and was replaced by a fresh faced Aucklander, Sean Fitzpatrick. But while we were working hard, there was very little fluidity. Both backs and forwards were pretty disjointed, largely because we weren't familiar with each other's play.

Then, on Friday night, David Kirk ran the captain's meeting at the hotel. Kirky began by talking about what it meant to play for New Zealand, what it meant to your family, the fact you were carrying the whole tradition of New Zealand rugby with you, and the importance of success in your own role, and as a team.

Then he asked the handful of guys who had played test rugby in the past to speak, John Kirwan, Arthur Stone and Brian McGrattan. Kirky kept moving it round the room, and one by one we all talked about our positions, and our feelings about the game.

The atmosphere just cranked up and up. It was a mixture of excitement about wanting to get out there and play, and apprehension about whether we'd succeed or fail as a team. I've never experienced anything as intense in a team meeting since. Guys were in tears. It was just fever pitch. I've said to friends later that if you'd suspended a match in midair in that room, it would have ignited.

Next morning it was all pretty quiet, but when we got to the changing room at Lancaster Park, the intensity was all there again. I was crying, and when I looked at Joe Stanley, Gordie

Macpherson, Brent Harvey, so were they. I think most of the team were actually sobbing. It was hard to come out of the room because we were crying so much.

Then when we ran out onto the field, you could just feel the whole team jell together. Suddenly I just had an incredible feeling of confidence about the side. You just knew that we were going to smash these French over.

Brian Lochore, and the four test players we had in the side, had all told us how swiftly the match would go. BJ (Lochore) had said, "You're all physically fit enough, you just need to prepare mentally. That'll take you through the game."

I started to feel tired in the first half, and it worried me because I was sure we'd only played 10 minutes. When I looked at the clock it was only two minutes to halftime.

In the forwards the French scrum was very good. They put us under a lot of pressure, and really dominated us there. But we managed to scramble things away, Frano Botica kept the ball ahead of us, and Arthur Stone and Joe Stanley were knocking them down in the midfield.

Very early in the game we got a great psychological boost from Greg Cooper, our fullback. The French spun it wide and brought in an extra man. We were playing a man on man defence in those days, and their winger, Patrice Lagisquet, had Greg to beat. Greg took him at bootlace level, and our forwards got there so quickly they blew in over the top and secured the ball. As soon as we saw that tackle we felt we had a man behind us who could do the job. We just got stronger and stronger, and eventually frustrated them into ill discipline.

Halfway through the first half Frano hoisted a kick, JK made a great burst, Brent Harvey took the pass, and passed infield to me. In my first test I scored my only test try.

I can remember very little of the second half, just making a lot of tackles, and hitting a lot of rucks as we kept the French out of the game, and won 18-9.

Just how much emotional energy had poured into that buildup was obvious that night. We were all just shattered. Personally I think I was asleep by 10pm, I was so drained. We'd made the ego-free climb, as short and quick as it was, and I was personally so innocent (or naive) I flew back to Dunedin the next morning and played for Otago against Taranaki.

The amazing electricity of the Christchurch success would soon be dampened. We all knew that the Cavaliers would be available for the last two tests against the Wallabies, so when we went to Wellington for the first, there was a little ill feeling in the side. Despite the victory in Christchurch we knew that if the new boys failed, they'd quickly bring in the old brigade.

Wellington didn't go well from the start. Our flight up from Dunedin was delayed, and Gordie Macpherson and I were just arriving at the hotel as the team was heading out for training. BJ told us to hurry and catch up.

At that stage Gordie had to strap his ankles every time he trained or played. I said to him, "Make sure you strap your ankles." Being the conscientious guy he is, and hating being late for training as much as I do, he said, "Shit no, we're late as it is."

Sure enough, he went up in the second lineout, came down, and rolled his ankle. He was out of the test, and would never play another one.

It was upsetting for the team, and it was especially upsetting for me. He was a good friend, and one of the most honest, hard working team men I've ever played with.

In the game at Athletic Park things didn't go too well either. In the end we could have won it, but we lost by one point, 13-12. We probably deserved to win that test more than the second in Dunedin. My only memories of the Wellington test are of how gut wrenching it was. You just felt hollow, knowing that they'd probably drop most of us.

Sure enough, they axed the whole forward pack, and two of the backs, for Dunedin. Buck Shelford took my position at No 8. Then Buck's bad luck became my good luck. He broke bones in his hand playing club rugby, so I was back in the team.

There's been talk since of divisions inside the All Blacks in 1986, especially between David Kirk, who refused to tour South Africa, and the Cavaliers.

The only time I was aware of it was late in the year, when we were touring France. I walked into Kirky's room, and he and Mark Shaw were having a real go. I was a 21-year-old fresh into the All Blacks, and I didn't even stop to find out exactly what was going on. I was just out of there.

With hindsight there must have been friction between some of the Cavaliers and Kirky. But for a start BJ Lochore was such a good coach, and so well respected, that he helped keep the side together. Also I think the players were all man enough to put aside the disagreements when it came to pulling on that black jersey and playing for New Zealand. Nothing mattered more than giving your last drop for the All Blacks. Today if there's a wee bit of animosity between players it can get carried onto the field.

In '86 there was also an expectation that younger players would work to earn the respect of senior players. I don't see anything wrong with that, although some young players now seem to feel that if they show a bit of brilliance, they should be treated and respected like some of the senior players from day one.

During my first couple of years, like other young players then, you just wanted to keep out of the way, and hopefully have the senior players accept you because they thought you'd done the hard work they had to get there.

The first time I got on the team bus before the second Wallabies test in Dunedin I went to sit in the third seat on the left from the front.

"Get out of there," said a gruff voice (I think it was Mark Shaw). "Axle'll rip your throat out." Axle was Gary Knight, a huge prop, who had also represented New Zealand as a wrestler.

So I lurked around the front of the bus until every other player had sat down. Only then did I slide into an empty seat.

I kept very quiet around Axle in the changing room before the test too. We arrived at Carisbrook about 50 minutes before the game, and dropped our bags in the changing room. I like to go out and have a look at the ground, but as soon as he came in Axle took off his blazer, took off his tie, and lay down on the bench.

After five minutes looking at the Brook we came back in, and

Axle was still lying there. I got undressed, put some liniment on my legs, and some Vaseline over the top to try to keep the warmth in. Axle was still lying there.

I started to get a bit worried. There were only 20 minutes to go, and he looked like he was asleep. I whispered to Greg Cooper, "What's going on here? Is this guy going to play or what?"

Then, with just 10 minutes to go he stood up, shook himself, let out a bellow like a big bear, and started ripping off his shirt and trousers. He flung on his rugby gear, and "boof", he was out the door onto the field. Apparently that was the way he always prepared.

We were lucky to win the test, 13-12. Steve Tuynman scored a try that the referee disallowed. I couldn't believe it wasn't awarded.

When we went to Auckland for the last test we struck a style of play that Alan Jones brought in, and Bob Dwyer has continued with the Wallabies to this day.

Basically their game plan is to kick it long, but not out. You force the opposition to kick the ball out, and you have very tall locks, like Skylab Cutler, Bill Campbell, and John Eales to win the lineout for you. Their jumpers are lanky and thin, so they go a lot to four and five man lineouts to make sure they're not interfered with. Their game is still based on that.

A lot of people say the Wallabies move the ball a lot, but really they're like Auckland. They don't run the ball until they've got points up, and dominance up front. Until then their game is quite constrained.

In the third test at Eden Park in '86 we realised the Wallabies would kick long, so we aimed to counter attack from everywhere, rather than kick the ball out. We failed dismally.

They were a lot fitter than us. It was very noticeable from the first training after they returned that the Cavaliers were not as fit as the Baby Blacks had been. In Dunedin and Auckland we did a lot more talking than actual hard work. When players started blowing a bit they'd stop and discuss things for five minutes.

When we ran the ball they had the fitness to keep knocking us over. A perfect example was when Hika Reid was charging for the goalline, and Enrique Rodriguez just lined him up and drilled him. That was the story of the game. When we tried to counter attack they hit us hard, and we coughed the ball up. In the end they did the running and the scoring, and we lost 22-9.

When the team was named for the tour to France at the end of the year Buck was back, and Jock Hobbs was the captain. It seemed to me that the likely loose forward trio was Buck at No 8, Jock on the openside, and Mark "Cowboy" Shaw on the blindside. My aim before the tour was to try to put as much pressure as I could on Buck and Cowboy for a test spot.

It seemed likely I'd only get two games before the test, and the first, at Clermont-Ferrard, was a muddly sort of match, so I thought, "That's one chance blown." Then after my second game in Perpignan I got the next game too, in Bayonne. Cowboy was in the Bayonne game also. I really tried to get another good one in, and things went okay.

But I was still stunned when I was selected ahead of Cowboy for the first test. He must have been disappointed, but he was the first one to come up to me.

"Congratulations, son," he said. "But remember, when you wear this jersey and want to play test matches, you've got to be prepared to piss blood."

I have a lot of respect for Cowboy. On that tour he often took the dirty dirties (the guys not needed as players or reserves for the next game) training, and he pushed himself right to the limit.

He had a philosophy that the dirties trained harder than the playing XV, because you weren't getting the benefit of the game. It's easy if you find yourself playing the midweek games to fall into the trap of not playing hard enough to put pressure on the Saturday team.

It takes a player like Cowboy to urge the midweek team to play and train hard, to lift their own performances so they're not only winning the midweek games, but challenging for the Saturday team. And it was also part of Cowboy's character that if he didn't make the Saturday side he was still right in there supporting it.

The French tour was very hard physically. In the Cote d' Basque game in Bayonne before the first test I remember being booted right in the base of the spine. I had deep, black bruising from there, down my bum, and into my hamstrings. In almost every game, if you were on the ground you were stood on. I think I was stitched after every game, and so were many of the other forwards.

If the New Zealand public saw rugby on television the way it was played in France in 1986 there would have been citings after every game for all eight French forwards.

We won the first test in Toulouse, 19-7, and then played the second, and final, test in Nantes.

This was a game that was vital to their coach, Jacques Foroux. A bit like Bob Dwyer in his early days with the Wallabies, Foroux's coaching career with France was always on a knife edge. Apparently Foroux had been close to being sacked several times, and France had to win the second test for him to be their coach at the World Cup.

Like Buck Shelford, I have rarely seen a team with eyes as glassy as the French players were in Nantes. In fact, there are only two occasions I'd compare to it. Once was watching, on television, the All Blacks in Paris in 1977, when they looked super charged. The other was the Waikato team in the first division final in Hamilton in 1992.

We'll never know if any of those teams were artificially stimulated, but I do know that the French began in Nantes like wildmen.

When they kicked off, the ball landed about 10 metres away from me. Someone, possibly Eric Champ, hit me so hard I was absolutely flattened. You knew immediately it was going to be all on.

The game was just so intense that it wasn't until we got home and Dad said to me, "You got hammered in the second test," and I watched a video that I realised they dominated us for the whole game. On the field it was only when we lost Gary Whetton, and then Buck Shelford, that I started to think we were going to struggle to win. Even then I didn't feel we were out of it.

Buck, who finally had to leave the field halfway through the second half with a split scrotum, had impressed me enormously on the whole tour. When things got tougher in a game he took another step forward into the confrontation. He was incredible to play with.

I spent a lot of time on the ground in France trying to clean up. That was the way we played in Otago. I lost count of the number of times that, bang, Buck would be on top of me, covering my butt so to speak. Buck's actually a soft natured individual, but when he's playing rugby he has a very hard attitude, and he hates being a loser. He's one of those people who will put his body through extreme pain to win.

The French were just too much to handle in Nantes, and we lost 16-3. It was intensely physical, although I wouldn't say it was that dirty. It was just that when you were hit, you were really hit. We had three days in Singapore on the way home, but when we got back to New Zealand I could still feel the aches and pains from the test.

Just ahead were some of the most glorious years in the ego-free climb of the All Blacks.

2

Into the Golden Weather

My first hint that the World Cup of 1987 would produce a new world star came on the Barbarians tour to Britain at the start of the year.

We played five matches there, and in the first game, against Leicester, I was on the openside, AJ Whetton was on the blindside, and Michael Jones, the man the selectors hadn't wanted in the Colts of '85, was at No 8.

It was about 20 minutes into the game when Michael took an in-pass from one of our threequarters, I think Craig Green. As he got the ball Michael was being crowded by the opposing centre, with Dusty Hare, an international fullback, closing on him too.

As he pushed off the centre Michael dropped the ball onto his foot, chipped it over Hare, ran round him, caught the ball on the full and dived over the line.

When you're running five metres infield the impression that sort of brilliance leaves on you is very vivid. AJ and I were backing up inside Michael, and I remember saying to AJ as Michael scored, "Who IS this guy?"

The tour as a whole was a great buildup to the World Cup. We were coached by former All Blacks Peter Murdoch and Kevin Barry, and while we played hard off the field, we were successful on it, finishing an unbeaten tour with a big win over the British Barbarians.

Back home they played zonal matches for trials, and I started getting what seemed to be a groin strain. Finally, in the trial in Ashburton, I ground to a halt. It felt like a motor seizing up, in my pelvic area. It tightened up that much that as soon as I tried to stretch out, it was agony. Tight forwards were running past me.

I left the field, and the next day X-rays revealed that I had a stress fracture of the pubic synthesis. I tried to give it some rest, but eventually it would mean six months off.

For a week I stayed in Christchurch while Brian McKenzie, who had been a physio with the All Blacks, gave me intensive treatment. My pelvis was about 5mm out of alignment from one side to the other. Brian put it back in place, and then it was put in plaster.

There doesn't seem to be any special reason why some players have the problem. A little halfback, Paul McGahan, has suffered from it, and so has a big flanker, Jamie Joseph.

Overuse is probably an issue, and perhaps a muscle imbalance. It might be genetic. Since recovering I've never had any more trouble from it, but I do try to keep the pelvic girdle well stretched now.

I was disappointed when I made my final decision that I wasn't available for the World Cup, but I've never been one to dwell on not making a side, basically because I've had other interests outside the game, whether it was university or work.

The All Blacks of '87 were playing the game at a different level to the other teams at the World Cup. As far as goal setting, skill levels, fitness levels and style of game, the All Blacks were in a different stratosphere.

As a team the All Blacks had set themselves individual goals, and goals as a group. Brian Lochore, Grizz Wyllie and John Hart had the team focused on one thing, to play a brand of rugby that they knew would be too strong, and too fast, for every other side in the world. They really went through to win the title uncontested.

When my injury finally allowed me to start training again I got a call from John Hart, who had been appointed to take an

All Black team to Japan at the end of the New Zealand season.

He said, "I'd like to take you as an openside flanker. We aren't taking Michael (Jones) because of the Sunday games up there." They weren't taking many of the older players, which meant Joe Stanley wasn't in the side, which disappointed me. I was lucky enough to be picked, and ended up playing all five games in Japan.

The games on tour were difficult, but the team did carry on from the World Cup. In training and in the matches the intensity came from the fact nobody wanted to make mistakes. It's one thing to play easy opponents, and run up big scores, but it's another to keep your intensity, and there were some matches in Japan where I don't think we made a single mistake.

In France the previous year the philosophy had been more "rip into it" with players like Cowboy Shaw and Hika Reid and those guys. But in '87 it was speed, skill and precision, at training and in a game, which I found quite refreshing.

It was a style of rugby I thoroughly enjoyed, and a style that had been too good for some of the major rugby nations in the world. Poor old Japan got 100 points put around them.

This was the tour that probably cost Harty his chance to be the All Black coach through to the next World Cup.

In Japan, Harty was the coach and Grizz was the assistant coach. Malcolm Dick, the Auckland Rugby Union chairman, was the manager, and two of Harty's friends from the Barbarians in Auckland, Peter Murdoch and Alan Rear, helped out in an unofficial capacity.

Apparently the perception of some council members was that Harty and Malcolm Dick were staging an Auckland takeover of the All Blacks. As someone from outside Auckland that wasn't a view I shared.

In fact I found the leap up in skill level and attitude from '86 to '87 quite astounding. Harty pushed the players hard at training, but he was innovative, motivational, and he got the best out of us. It suited me.

And it certainly didn't worry me that he was from Auckland, with an Auckland manager, and two other Aucklanders tagging along. I knew Peter Murdoch from the Barbarians tour to Britain, and he and Alan Rear were great guys. They fitted in well, and I don't believe the "Auckland takeover" bothered other players either.

Grizz was officially the assistant coach, but he had so little to do on the tour, I can hardly recollect his face there, that's how dominant Harty's role was.

One thing I do respect about Grizz is that he knew it was Harty's tour, and Harty's baby. If things went well, Harty got the credit. If not he took the fall. Grizz only stepped in and helped when he was wanted.

I do believe that when Harty was in the assistant's position with Grizz, four years later, he should have adopted a similar attitude, and let the guy who was the coach run the ship the way he wanted to. But it's not in Harty's nature to do that.

At the end of '87 the New Zealand council appointed Grizz the coach, and Harty dropped off the panel for a year, initially deciding that if he couldn't be in charge he didn't want to be involved at all.

All I knew of Grizz was that he was this gruff, grumpy bugger who really trained his teams hard. Andy Earl – Worzel – told some terrible stories about what Grizz would sometimes put the Canterbury side through on Sunday mornings, with guys throwing up on the training paddock.

At the same time, we also heard from Canterbury players that the camaraderie built up in Grizz's Ranfurly Shield squad was quite amazing. Several of the Cantabrians said it was the best team spirit they'd ever experienced.

When the side was picked to go to Australia in '88 the test loose forward trio was going to be Buck Shelford, who captained the side, AJ Whetton and Michael Jones. I was really trying to play as well as I could to get into the first test, which was on a Sunday.

I didn't mind what position, but with Michael's beliefs openside flanker was the obvious one. Zinzan Brooke was pushing for a spot as well, but he was more in competition with Buck.

Things went okay until the last match before the test, against

New South Wales Country. With about 20 minutes to go I tore a cartilage in my knee, which swelled up. I thought the test chance had gone.

But when the test team was named, I was in, as the openside flanker. My knee was still locking up on me a bit, so I went to John Mayhew, the All Black doctor, for a jab. He was using a long lasting local anaesthetic which he injected behind the knee to kill the pain.

On the Saturday he injected me, but when I went out for some lineout drills my foot kept rolling over. I had to stop. I was about to damage my ankle.

I went to Doc and asked him what was going on. He said he must have hit a nerve with the needle, and the nerve that triggered the muscle fibres was numbed. So all the muscles down the outside of my leg were not working.

It wasn't going to be a problem, said Doc, he'd just go in a bit further from the back of the knee. Came the test, and the knee was fine. We had a good win, 32-7, a hiding really, and I was more than happy with how I went.

Now I wanted to put as much pressure as I could on Michael to keep the spot. The next weekend our game against Queensland was again on a Sunday.

The knee was just about right, but I decided to have another jab to make sure. I wanted another big game, to keep the heat on, in the hope of making the second test.

Twenty minutes before the game Doc injected me again. We ran out to play Queensland, who some people said were stronger than the Wallabies, and my foot started going to sleep.

I said to Buck, "I can't keep going."

Buck asked, "Why? What's wrong?"

"My foot's asleep."

Reasonably enough, Buck was startled.

"What the hell are you talking about?"

"It's my foot Buck, it's asleep, and I keep rolling over on my ankle."

Buck wanted a quick repair. He told me, "Strap it up."

We stopped play while I took off my boot, and strapped up

the outside of my sock. We had another lineout. My foot rolled again.

"Buck, it's still asleep. It's hopeless."

He said, "Do something else."

This time we strapped the outside of the boot. I was starting to look more like an injured skier than a rugby player.

I went to Buck again. "I've got to go. It'll be like this for four hours, until the injection wears off."

Reluctantly I left the field, thinking any chance of the second test had just vanished.

Poor old Doc was beside himself. He was upset for me, and he was also concerned about the coach, who hadn't been told about the painkiller.

When I was changed Doc muttered to me, "What the hell are we going to tell Grizz?" I had no real ideas. "We'll dream something up."

It was a really tough game, but the boys hung in, and won. I was coming out of the changing room after the game as Grizz was coming in. He fixed me with one of those famous looks that can melt barbed wire.

"What the hell's the matter with you?" he asked.

"Do you want to know the truth?"

"Of course I bloody do."

"My foot's asleep."

He looked at me in total disbelief, mumbled "f***in' idiot" and walked away. I do believe that if we'd lost, the questions would have gone on for a lot longer.

Andy Earl had replaced me against Queensland and played very well. We then went to Townsville to play a night game against Queensland B. Both Michael and I played. I knew it was my only chance, and although I got cut above both eyes and needed stitches, I thought I'd played well enough to have a chance at the test.

Michael had been playing okay, but not up to the sublime level that he had in the World Cup. I half expected he'd get the nod, but before the team was announced John Sturgeon, the manager, came to me to tell me I hadn't made it.

I asked Sturgie why Grizz hadn't told me. He said Grizz had called it the hardest decision he'd had to make as far as test selection went. At the end of the tour I went to Grizz himself and said, "Why didn't you come and tell me yourself? You know I would have accepted it and supported you and the team." He said the same thing, "I couldn't tell you myself."

That was probably the first time I saw under the gruff exterior of Grizz Wyllie, to see that under the skin he wasn't a ruthless, grumpy person at all, but actually quite a soft centred guy. He found making a decision like that harder than anyone could imagine.

My attitude to being selected for a test has never changed. You bust your guts to get in the squad, but if you miss out, hard luck. If you're lucky enough to get into the reserves, there's a chance you'll get on the paddock. If you're a dirty dirty, not in the team, or the reserves, you're in there supporting the team.

We almost lost the second test, and I remember it for the only time I ever saw Joe Stanley beaten on the outside. Joe was caught when, just for a split second, he thought Johnny Schuster was going to miss his man. Joe turned to cover Michael Cook on the inside, and he slipped the pass to James Grant.

Joe's never forgotten that moment, which illustrates how even a complete player like him can be beaten if he loses confidence for an instant in the man alongside him. A team becomes great when everyone has total confidence in every player in the side.

Down 16-6 at halftime, the boys dragged themselves back to snatch a 19-all draw. Foxy missed a conversion right on fulltime, and blamed himself for the team missing the win. But to my mind it showed the calibre of the side that they could even come back to have a chance at the death at all.

In the drink session after the test Grizz had been as grumpy as hell (I said he found telling a player bad news hard, not letting a team know they hadn't played to expectations).

As we were leaving the drink session he said, "Right, make sure you take your training gear with you on the plane to Sydney. We'll have training as soon as we get off, and you won't have time to get it out of your suitcases."

27

We all thought we were going to get hammered. We flew to Sydney, got our gear, and went across the bridge in a bus to T.G. Milner Park in Terrogal.

Reluctantly we changed into our jerseys and shorts and socks, and as we sort of milled round outside the clubrooms (there was a club game going on), Grizz said, "Go in and take your shorts off, and put on your No 1 trousers and shoes." We were too numb to work out what was going on.

When we changed Grizz yelled, "Righto, follow me", and he stormed into the clubhouse where this huge booze-up had been organised. There were 12oz glasses lined up in a big circle, and we basically kept going until we fell over.

I remember a big wrestling, thumping, fight on the bus as the players up the front attacked the back seat. I don't really remember crashing, but I do remember waking up in the hotel in Gosford on the Monday morning still in the footie jersey and long trousers.

In the end it was a great thing. It blew the drawn game out of everyone's systems, and the boys started to focus on the last test, where Michael Jones had one of his best games of the tour, and we blitzed the Wallabies again.

On reflection, even though I missed out on the last two tests, it was one of the most enjoyable tours I've ever been on, along with the '89 tour. Normally, if I'd gone on tour, and only played one test out of three, I'd regard it as a bit of a failure personally, but that was overcome by the intensity and atmosphere in Australia.

We didn't have two teams of 15, we had one team of 30, and regardless of who was playing, the whole team focused on winning. To become a great team you must have team unity and in Australia we had all the members concentrating on one goal.

Australia is also a very comfortable country for New Zealanders to tour. We're at ease, and even though there's really not that much difference between a three hour plane trip, or a 12 hour plane trip, away from home, you do feel much closer when you're in Australia. You normally enjoy good weather, with firm grounds, which isn't the case in most northern hemisphere winters.

Let's also give credit to the Australians, who I believe are consistently the only team we play who go out to play their own game. By comparison, the British, even the French, play a containing style of rugby, aiming to score their tries from counter attacking.

The Wallabies and the All Blacks try to force their style of play from set pieces, trying whenever possible, to attack, rather than playing a basically defensive type of game. That's another thing that makes Australia so enjoyable to tour.

When we got back from Australia, one of the first provincial games we had was against North Harbour at the Onewa Domain. Doc Mayhew, a North Harbour man, and I had a bet in Australia for half a dozen bottles of port on the outcome.

I had a chat with Laurie, and our plan revolved around blowing the Harbour scrum back, which would make it difficult for Buck, their man mountain, ikon, and No 8 to run off the back of the scrum, which he did so well for them. It worked. Their scrum was going back all day, we were able to knock Buck over, and my only regret was that some of our rucking went a bit over the top, with Buck needing stitches to his head. We won the match 15-13.

In the New Zealand summer of '88-'89 I was in Italy, playing club rugby with Frano Botica, and there was a certain amount of fuss over some of us arriving back late for the final trial, in May. Frano and I played in a Possibles side against a shadow test team in Hamilton, and he was brilliant. We almost tipped over the Probables, finally going down 31-25.

I wasn't in the squad for two tests against France, and then two against Argentina, but in Napier, with Otago, watched the second Argentinean test on TV, and saw the horrific leg injury suffered by Michael Jones. As Joe Stanley said, it was a freak accident that wouldn't have happened to most players, because most players wouldn't have been trying to gently push the ball past an opponent with the aim of swooping round to pick it up.

Because of Michael's injury, which it seemed initially might end his career, I was in the side to play a Bledisloe Cup test against the Wallabies at Eden Park. The test was tough and tense, with the Aussies in striking distance until the last 10 minutes, when we got out to 24-12. It was just a one-off test, but it was great to be back in the side.

At the end of our winter the team was named to tour Wales and Ireland, and at Carisbrook there was a small going-away function for Paul Henderson and myself (John Timu would join the tour when John Kirwan was injured).

I remember Eric Watson, the former All Black coach, saying to me, "You'll hate Wales."

It was the first time, after tours to France, England and Australia, that anyone had ever said anything like that to me. It made an impact, especially coming from someone who had coached a team there.

"What do you mean, Eric?"

He said, "Well, if you think the New Zealand public are mad about rugby, wait until you get to Wales. They're fervent. The rugby will be hard, and you won't enjoy their public off the field."

It isn't until you tour Wales, as an All Black, that you understand what he means. Ian Kirkpatrick, when he was captain of the All Blacks there in 1972, is supposed to have said, "You never beat Wales, you just have more points on the scoreboard."

We found his words so true.

The South Africa-New Zealand rivalry is intense, but really it's even stronger with the Welsh. For a Welshman, playing against the All Blacks is the highpoint of his career. From the time we arrived no matter what you won by, there was always an excuse. "Just wait till you get to the valleys, boyo," someone would tell us, "We'll kick the shite out of you."

In our first match, against Cardiff, we won only 25-15, and Buck said after the game, "Now we know how hard it's going to be."

Walking down the street with a couple of other players a boy about 10 walked past and said, "Hey, you're the All Blacks."

We thought he wanted an autograph, and said, "Yeah, we are."

Then he spat at our feet.

We were amazed. Being parochial is one thing, but this was right over the top.

We struggled our way through, with strange incidents dogging us all the way. The crowd in Neath jostled the referee after the game, and we were all just glad to get out of it. In Llanelli there was the ridiculous situation with Joe Stanley and Andy Earl spending the night in a cell, after they'd defended themselves against an attack at our pub. In Newport the local team went down to their 22 when we did our haka, so Buck led the team over the halfway line to challenge them. With the terrible weather, and the Welsh media getting into us a bit, the whole feeling wasn't great.

When it came to the test, I think the Welsh thought they'd have a really good crack at us because we hadn't performed as well as we had in '87 and '88.

It was Graeme Bachop's first test, and Craig Innes' first test. The first time Bach got the ball he put up a beautiful kick into the box and Postie (Innes) came through and smashed the left wing, Arthur Emyr, over. We got a scrum, and Postie came off the blindside wing, and scored really early.

From then on we totally dominated the game. It was a really good test. We were too intense, too fast and too skilled for them. In the end we gave them a good old fashioned hiding, 34-9. They were just devastated, but we were really happy, not just because we'd won the test, but also because we were getting out of Wales and were going to Ireland.

It's a sad twist that if you tour Wales as an All Black supporter, you have a ball. The people are very hospitable and New Zealanders following the team get treated extremely well.

If you're a player it's different. You enjoy the competitive nature of the games, but you feel constantly under scrutiny, and you basically get a hard time.

We found it so refreshing to know we were going to Ireland. It would have been a tragedy if we'd gone to Ireland first, and finished the tour in Wales.

After the test in Cardiff we had an absolutely huge night. New Zealand Breweries had sent over mountains of their products, and I can still see trays and trays of Steinlager and Lion Red that we were told we wouldn't be able to take to Ireland with us. We partied away the frustrations of the Welsh section of the tour, and some managed as much as an hour's sleep before we staggered onto a Ryanair plane to go to Dublin.

One of the attendants on that flight is now my wife. It's a matter of some amazement to friends that the first time Bev and I saw each other I was virtually in a comatose state. I did stay awake long enough to notice she was very attractive, and to think Bev and the other hosties must have thought we were a bunch of drunks. We reeked of alcohol.

Luckily the chance to meet Bev would come when I was in a more civilised condition, and on the football front the Irish tour was a pleasure too.

The Irish lack nothing in heart and intensity when they play the game, but they do lack some of the basic skills to compete consistently at the top level. If a team's not on song, or they haven't prepared well, then through the sheer ruggedness of their approach, the Irish can put you off your stride.

But we'd been through a gruelling tour of Wales, and we had the fitness to use all the skills in the team. After three relatively easy wins we were never pressed in the test match, even if a zealous touch judge did deprive Foxy of his first test try.

Ireland had been a superb way to end the tour. The way they approached the game, and the generous-spirited attitude of the public was a wonderful chance after the much grimmer time we had in Wales.

Inside the team it was a happy tour. It's only in hindsight that you could see signs of the wheels starting to wobble on the All Black machine, after three glorious years on the fast track.

3

The Plague Years

I've never been so wild at the end of a game. When the referee, Steve Hilditch, blew his whistle for fulltime I jumped out of my seat and stalked out of the grandstand. Bev, and even some people in the group of supporters we were travelling with, were worried about me. They could see I was seething.

On the field, at Cardiff Arms Park, the All Blacks' World Cup campaign for 1991 had just finished. On a bleak October afternoon New Zealand had beaten Scotland 13-6 for third place. Some critics saw signs of hope for the future in the victory. I was disgusted.

During the game Steve McDowell, Sean Fitzpatrick, even Richard Loe, who had formed the best front row in world rugby, were hanging round the back of rucks and mauls, looking for a run with the ball, or just a rest. Gary Whetton, such a great lock for New Zealand for 11 seasons, had gone to ground once, and then just sat there for 10 or 15 seconds, watching play move downfield away from him, before getting up to follow the ball.

For my taste it was the bitter end of an era. What could be called "the plague of selfishness" had eaten into the All Blacks. They were no longer a team the rest of the world struggled to just stay in touch with. Now it was the All Blacks doing the struggling.

The "plague of selfishness" occurs within a team when a small group of the elite players want the major share of the acclaim and rewards. Instead of thinking what they can do for the team, they ask what the team can do for them. Some players feel they're under-appreciated, so cliques and rivalries can form very easily. It is easy to become selfish, even inside a team. The hardest thing for a player in a team to do is to reach a stage where the sacrifice being made is for the betterment of the team, not just for the individual.

Part of the plague to my mind, involves players, especially those who feel they've made a major contribution to the success already achieved by the team, looking for an easy way to do things. That's human nature, but it can be fatal to a rugby team's success.

Where did the trouble start with the All Blacks? How had we gone from a team that was unrelenting, playing a game of continuity football that left other teams gasping, to a side where some of our best players were trying to catch a breather whenever they could?

Like most organisations, the problems didn't appear overnight, they gradually got bigger and bigger until they could no longer be papered over. And at the heart of the difficulties was a very old fashioned reason: The All Blacks were not fit enough.

At the same time the All Blacks were having the triumphs of 1987 and 1988, the Auckland team had become so dominant in New Zealand rugby that no other provincial team could even get close to taking the Ranfurly Shield off them. The individual players were just so good.

Their fitness expert was Jim Blair, who began with Canterbury, and then became involved with the All Blacks, as well as Auckland. He'd done a lot of research with American Football in the 1980s, and his philosophy changed the way training was run towards the end of the decade.

I remember him being quoted as saying that Auckland and All Black prop Steve McDowell didn't have to run when he was training for rugby, Steve was using judo and gym work. Jim said the same thing about Ian Jones, that he didn't want Ian pounding the roads. Jim was quoted as saying: "The bulk of a forward's job on the field is really physically contesting the ball against his opposite number, in scrums, mauls and lineouts. When you run on the road, the bulk of the effect is in your legs. I want it throughout the whole body. So I prefer things like circuit work in the gymnasium."

Those theories went directly against my views, formed from a background in physical education. Specificity of training, I had learned, was all important. In other words, if you're a cyclist, you have to cycle, if you're a swimmer, you have to swim. If you're a rugby player the basic component of your game is running around a field. Therefore, you have to run.

Inside the All Blacks you formed the opinion that senior Auckland players were pushing Jim into finding an easier way to train, so they didn't have to slog it out. That's where I think things were starting to break down.

As All Black coach Grizz Wyllie came from the old school, even though he'd worked with Jim for Canterbury. Grizz agreed with the Arthur Lydiard philosophy of training. To be able to perform at peak levels for endurance events, the athlete needs a very strong aerobic base. This gives the athlete strength and endurance, the essential elements for success.

That didn't sit easily with some of the senior players from Auckland, who started to complain about what they saw as Grizz's antiquated methods of training. They felt there was too much hard work in the Grizz way, running and running and hitting tackle bags, until you were buggered, and then running some more.

But by 1989 Jim was the guru, and he was saying you don't have to hurt in training. He said he based the theories on the NFL, on the way they trained American footballers. Most of their training, which is very specialised, and very effective, revolves around power and explosiveness. The trouble is that the dynamics of the sports - rugby and American football - are totally different.

In rugby union the players, especially the forwards, are playing an aerobic based sport, where sustained effort is required. But American football is anaerobic. Play stops and starts all the time, with relatively lengthy rest periods in between. I actually think American football training would work better in league than in union. The dynamics of their game is much closer to the NFL.

Let me explain a little further. To keep going in a sport for 80 minutes means the sport is basically aerobic. An anaerobic sport is one where you're performing for less than three minutes. So even a 1500 metre race or a mile run in under four minutes is still very definitely based on aerobic training.

When I was a kid I was a big John Walker fan, and I read *Kiwis Can Fly*, a book that explained how Walker, Dick Quax and Rod Dixon could last the European athletics season and still be so successful. It came down to the mileage they put into their legs and their bodies. If you don't have that base then at the end of a 1500 metres race, when the rest of the field is kicking for home, you won't have the strength to compete. My whole basis of preparation is that if you haven't done the miles you won't be there at the finish.

Even Bart Cummings, one of the best ever Melbourne Cup horse trainers, says much the same thing. In his words, "If you don't put the miles into the legs, the horse won't have the mile at the end." It's exactly the same philosophy.

As time went by I had some fairly lengthy discussions (well, to be honest, they were more like arguments) with Grizz over our training. I even talked with John Hart, a big Jim Blair supporter, over it. I told Grizz: "I totally disagree with what we're doing for fitness. We're trying to cut the corners, take the short cuts. In the end it'll fall over. In the past the All Blacks have always won in the last 20. Now we'll start to lose in the last 20."

Let me be fair about Jim Blair. The very good things that he brought to New Zealand rugby were the skills and drills, especially the grids at training. Jim Blair really brought grid training into world rugby. When you're running grids, balls are being passed at speed, while players are running on what could be collision courses. Peripheral vision, concentration, and the elimination of errors are all enhanced, which are rugby specific skills. John Hart was especially good at using those drills, which revolutionised training, and kept it interesting and fun. But it was probably Jim more than anyone who made them part of rugby. He looked at what they do in British soccer, adapted the methods to rugby, and changed the way we look at a training session in New Zealand.

They made an enormous difference to the skill levels of all the players, from fullback to the front row. They could all handle the ball and not make mistakes. The classic example would have been Steve McDowell. In the past, with very few exceptions, international props didn't run with the ball in hand. In '87, '88 and '89 look at how dominant Steve became running with the ball.

So there was nothing wrong with the skill training we were doing. Where we started to miss the bus was in the fitness work, and the best skills in the world are no use if you're too exhausted to use them.

As early as his second season as All Black coach, in 1989, there was certainly pressure starting to come on Grizz from the Auckland players to start to change his ways. Now the initial impression of Alex is that he has absolute confidence in himself, but I don't think that's the case. In fact, I think it's typical of someone whose inner self is not very confident to develop a gruff exterior to cover that fact.

Alex was very much like that when he had decisions to make with selections. He'd announce his decision in a very gruff manner and first the journalists, then the rest of New Zealand, would think, "Well, this guy knows what he's doing. He's certainly the boss, that's the way it's going to be." But internally there might have been conflict.

When he became All Black coach he initially presented himself to the players as a very tough, very demanding man. He really ran us hard. His great phrase during a training run was "on the line." When you heard him say that all the heads dropped a bit. You knew you were in for some really rugged work, and he didn't let you down.

But at the end of it, you knew it was good for you. It's typical of anything hard you have to do in life, whether it's training or work, you might hate having to do it, but once you've done it there's a real sense of satisfaction. Grizz had a lot of respect from the players for his past record, as a great player and coach for Canterbury, and the All Blacks initially were almost totally dominant. When a guy's that successful you don't question anything.

So in 1988 you had a coach players would have never thought to challenge, or query. But Alex is actually a coach who likes to get to know his players, and that's when players can start to turn a coach around. In retrospect, he probably didn't set new goals and new objectives to keep the players striving, and the game plan didn't evolve too much either.

Some of the players started getting a bit bored and tired with everything. The hard work that Grizz had brought himself and his teams up on just got too difficult. He was dealing with some very strong personalities in the All Blacks, Steve McDowell, Grant Fox, Gary and AJ Whetton, Sean Fitzpatrick, John Kirwan, and at that level you've got to keep things fresh, keep setting new goals, different targets. Otherwise the team will eventually fall over.

In the end we were not training as hard as we had been. As players like Steve got closer to Grizz they basically wore him down. They told him we didn't need all the hard work. Power and dynamic training would get us through. And perhaps Grizz, realising he was starting to lose a little of the confidence of the players, softened up a bit, instead of stepping aside from the players and just being himself. The real Alex Wyllie was an "on the line" man, but the longer he was All Black coach, the more frequent would be the occasions when we expected a real toughie of a training run, and it didn't eventuate.

In 1987-88-89 the whole All Black game was based around moving the ball wide and beating the opposition through continuity and support play. To do that we needed a really sound aerobic base. In that era we had it. We scored a lot of tries, and it didn't matter who scored them.

That style gradually eroded, because of our declining fitness levels, and also because "the plague of selfishness" was even starting to affect how players thought about the team. By now the profile of the All Blacks was sky high, and players were looking for personal rewards. We were starting to see the pass to a support player not being made, because there was a bit of the "if I score this try I'll be the movie star" attitude creeping in.

But when we played Scotland at the start of 1990 nobody would have expected the upheaval that was about to occur. The Dunedin test was a typical first up affair. The Scots came at us, and knocked us off our game, and although we won 31-16, we struggled to do so. Our problem was that even though we played badly, deep down we knew we could beat them if they got close. About the only memorable moment from Dunedin was that Kieran Crowley, back in the side after John Gallagher went to league, scored a great try, kicking over a tackler's head and catching the ball on the full.

The ultimatum was given that if we didn't perform at Eden Park a week later there would be changes when the Australians arrived for a three test tour. We struggled even more in the second test with Scotland.

In the end it came right down to a penalty from Foxy. At the time there was controversy over whether I'd played within the rules to get it. They'd just changed the offside rule regarding the 10 metre circle. Previously you had to be behind the kicker before chasing a kick upfield, or the kicker had to run past you to put you onside. The rule was changed so you could actually be 30 metres in front of the kicker, as long as you were 10 metres from the ball when it was retrieved. As soon as the defender moved five metres you could tackle them as long as you began 10 metres away from them. I watched on TV how the Aussie league players used the rule in their game. They'd start running downfield, stop 10 metres from the bounce, then make the tackle.

That's almost exactly what I did at Eden Park, where I was openside flanker, playing off the tail of the lineout. As soon as the ball was tapped off the top I knew Foxy was going to kick long, so I started sprinting deep. When he kicked the ball I was at least 30 metres in front of him. The ball came over my head, and Gavin Hastings, the Scottish fullback, caught it. I just stood still. Gavin hesitated. He was thinking, "What the hell's going on here? He's offside." As soon as he moved I went forward and tackled him. He didn't let the ball go, so we got the penalty, and Foxy got the three points. It was certainly within the rules, and we won 21-18.

It's traditional after a test for the loose forwards to get together and have a cigar and a port. After that test Buck Shelford, AJ Whetton and I were talking things over and we knew that heads were on the line.

But we were all quite happy with our games as loose forwards. On the field you know who is doing the work, and it was our opinion as loose forwards that our tight five, mostly because of how we were training, weren't performing the way they should have. Basically they didn't have that aerobic fitness, and they weren't dominating at the set pieces, or smashing into rucks and mauls.

As a loose forward trio we didn't feel we were getting the support of our tighties, and when the tight forwards aren't performing it's often the loose forwards who look bad. You're sucked into the tight work and it becomes more difficult to perform the roles of a loose forward, such as support play and getting quickly to the breakdown.

As we sipped our ports we agreed that I'd go, or AJ would go, or both of us would go. But we thought Buck would stay. He was playing well, doing the work that had to be done. He might not have been getting out as wide as you'd like him to, but that because he was having to do so much work in the tight.

Before the team was announced for the first test with Australia Steve Davie, a Dunedin journalist, rang me. He said, "Have you seen the team?" I said I hadn't. He said, "There's a change in the loose forwards." I basically thanked him for ringing, because I thought he was letting me know that I'd been dropped. But he said it wasn't me. I said, "Hell, AJ's been dropped." No, it's not AJ. "What?" He said, "Yeah, Wayne Shelford's been dropped." All I could say was, "You're bloody joking!"

I was just devastated for Buck. Their reasoning was that he wasn't getting wide enough, but they didn't look at the root cause. The tight forwards weren't performing.

I didn't know what to do, or what to say. "Bad luck" seemed so inadequate. So I didn't call Buck immediately. Looking back I wish I had. When JK got dropped three years later I called him straight away. It's desperately hard when someone you think should be in the team is dropped. For me with Buck it was even harder that it was a fellow loose forward, and an inspirational captain.

But the decision had been made. Gary Whetton was to be the captain against the Wallabies. Things were changing at the top, and it wasn't just with the captaincy.

After the way we trained for, and played in, the first test against the Wallabies in 1990 you would never have imagined what problems lay ahead for the All Blacks.

The whole atmosphere was very positive. Zinzan Brooke, who had replaced Buck at No 8, fitted in superbly, and we set scrum after scrum at training, because that was where we wanted to dominate Australia.

It worked. We commanded the scrums, we beat them 21-6, and personally I was able to range out wide, and really enjoy the day and the victory. Among the public and the media the suggestions were made that we didn't need Buck anymore.

But the euphoria started to evaporate in the second test, when the Wallabies lost by 10 points, and it was all gone by the third, at Athletic Park, when they won 21-9. Partly it was the fact of touring. The Aussies got fitter and fitter as their tour went on, and they had to redeem themselves in the last test to salvage anything from the visit.

By contrast our fitness levels were really starting to flag. We struggled just to get round the paddock. In 1988-89 we'd hunted as a pack. By 1990 we were arriving in dribs and drabs. There didn't seem to be the team unity.

Rumours started to fly about a fallout between Buck and Grant Fox. I didn't see, or know anyone else in the team who did, any of the things that were being suggested.

The reality was that on match day on the field during a game Foxy called most of the shots. He was in a pivotal position at first-five. If you're captaining the team from the forwards it's actually great to have a first-five who is almost dictatorial. But if there were any situations in a game where Buck wanted to keep it in the forwards, he would over-ride Foxy.

Everyone knew that when the captain made a decision he was the captain. No questions, you followed him. Buck was that kind of person too. He didn't say a lot on the field, but when he did you reacted immediately, because he led the charge. There were times when he and Foxy would disagree over tactics. Really it was just a natural phenomenon. There was certainly nothing dramatic about it. In the end it was like any other organisation, the guy in the chair makes the final decision. He's the one who has to face the consequences.

The arrival of Gary as captain didn't just signal a change in the on-field leadership. During Buck's era as captain Grizz did most of the talking at training. If players did speak up, even when Buck was captain, it was usually Gary or Foxy. Off the field there was no doubt though that Grizz had the authority and Buck was supporting him. From 1990 that began to change as John Hart, who had been reappointed as a selector in 1989, increasingly had more to say.

On the 1989 tour to Britain there were some strange undercurrents. Zinzan Brooke had been promised by Harty before the tour began that he would play at least one of the tests. Zinny told me that himself when we talked once about how close he had come to playing league for Manly. It wasn't a promise Zinny took that seriously. He knew that while Harty helped select the touring squad, once we were on tour Grizz was coaching, and selecting, without an assistant. There was very little Harty could do to influence the test selection.

But the tour in '89 had hardly started when Gary Whetton came to my hotel room in Swansea.

He said to me, "Look, we've got to have Zinny playing No 8 in the test matches."

I said, "What are you talking about?"

Gary replied, "Well, Zinny's form at home this season has been far superior to Buck's."

I agreed with that. As far as domestic form went Zinny had

been playing better than Buck. But I also said, "You've got to remember that Zinny has the benefit of having a dominant forward pack in front of him. And as far as I'm concerned Zinny has never performed at international level." On the 1988 tour of Australia, Zinny had never really threatened Buck for his position.

So I told Gary, "If anyone ever asks me, I'd give my opinion based purely on who's performing the best on tour. And there are still four or five matches to the Welsh test. I might want to have a crack at No 8 myself."

Gary walked to the door. "So we haven't got your support?"

I said, "No, you haven't."

It was a strange conversation, and it certainly wasn't just a casual remark or two. In all we spoke for about 10 minutes, and while Gary didn't seem angry about my position, I wouldn't have said he was happy either. Reading between the lines I must say I suspected that Harty was behind the visit. It was certainly, looking back, the first sign for me that eventually Alex would be eclipsed as All Black coach.

Harty is a very political creature, and I know for a fact that he's always on the phone to the Auckland players about the coaches, about the game plans. It happened when Grizz was the coach, it happened when Laurie Mains became coach.

My opinion is that he talks too much to the players when he's not coaching the team. He talks about what they're doing, what they're not doing. What they should be doing with the game plan. I think he ends up screwing up the guys a lot of the time, getting them mixed up.

For example, Harty was forever on the phone to John Kirwan. Now JK likes being buoyed up as a player, but if things aren't running his way, and he's got Harty on the phone telling him how well he's going, and then the man in charge starts knocking something JK's doing, some negativity must build up.

Basically Harty's attitude is just different from mine. I'm from the school that says if Jimmy Smith is the coach of an up and coming star, you don't try to get inside the brain of the star unless Jimmy Smith asks you to help out. Unless you're invited, you leave the player alone.

When we went to France at the end of 1990 it was a rebuilding exercise in many ways. We'd lost Frano Botica, Matt Ridge, John Gallagher and John Schuster to league, and early in the tour we found ourselves under some pressure as newcomers found their way into the team.

We struggled through the first five games, losing two of them. So going into the first test we were the underdogs, although we knew we hadn't put our best fifteen on the paddock before the test.

When it came to the test, a lot of the guys had been in the team hammered in '86 in Nantes, and the call was to 'Remember Nantes.' We knocked in two quick tries early, and basically ran over them that day, winning 24-3.

There were just two tests on the tour, and when we got to Paris Grizz bracketed Zinny and me. I'd played the first half in Nantes, then got a knock on the knee, and was replaced by Zinny.

At the first test squad training in Paris, Grizz said, "Righto, let's get going." He didn't say who the No 8 was.

I looked at Zinny, he looked at me, and in that second I just belted out onto the field and took up the position. Grizz didn't say anything, and I ended up training, and playing the test. I don't know that the side has been officially named to this day.

That was an odd one, but I actually think that in general Grizz used the tour very well. His objective was to win the tests, and he kept his cards up his sleeve through most of the games, to win the big prize. We took out the second 30-12.

Simon Mannix was one player who suffered from that tour. He was just a teenager, and he concentrated so hard on his rugby that he virtually burnt out. I often mention in speeches that it is important to keep a balance when on tour. You should enjoy some of the culture of the country you're visiting, because nothing but rugby every waking minute of the day is actually not the best recipe for success for most people.

We did better in France than we would in Argentina, or at the World Cup, which probably comes down to several factors. Revenge for Nantes was a major incentive, and after we'd thrashed France in the first test, they never really recovered. France was a more congenial country to tour than Argentina, and Grizz was still working us hard enough to get the team fitter as the tour went on.

After the second test you could start to feel a little bit of tension starting to build about the training, with some players complaining that the runs had been too hard and too long, which I thought was rubbish.

By the time we got to the start of 1991, and the tour to Argentina, some of the senior players were really starting to complain about Grizz. It was always going to be a difficult tour, and nobody was keen to go on it. The Argentineans played a spoiling style of game, and their referees were often a problem on their own. We went early in the year when their grounds were rock hard, and we all knew there was a big provincial season back home, with the World Cup late in the year.

It was in Argentina that senior players started using the excuse that Grizz was losing the plot, and that he was drinking too much. Grizz certainly enjoyed having a few beers, but so do a lot of sports people, especially rugby players. The idea of him going off the rails because of his drinking was just another excuse to oust him, and have John Hart running the side.

What was really happening was that as a group of guys we didn't want to do the hard work anymore. Almost from the first training run there were complaints about how long we trained, and suggestions that it wasn't really required.

My own tour was short. In my second game I had to leave the field against Tucuman, with a partial rupture of the plantar fascia, basically the sheath that holds the muscles under the foot onto the heel. When I tried to run there was a burning, almost tearing, sensation. There was no chance of a quick recovery.

The night before I was leaving for New Zealand I ended up going out for a beer with Grizz, and Steve McDowell came along. Now Steve was very much part of the group who wanted Grizz to lighten up on the trainings. As the night went on it got pretty heated between Steve and myself. Grizz went to the loo at one stage, and when he got back we were at it hammer and tongs, and then Grizz joined in.

I said to Grizz and Steve that we didn't have the aerobic fitness the team needed, that the players should stop making excuses for their own non-commitment, and if we didn't start working harder now it'd be too late by the time we got to the World Cup.

The next morning Grizz really got fired up. I wasn't flying out until the afternoon and he asked me to take the warm-up before training, and to make it hard. Then he virtually ran the boys into the ground. It was a rock hard field and they were really bitching and complaining. At that stage I could see we didn't have a happy camp in World Cup year. In fact you could see in Argentina what would eventually happen at the World Cup.

They complained about the training being boring and too hard. But my opinion was that the guys just didn't do the hard work in their own time in the off season. The thing is that when you are fit, it doesn't really matter what training sessions you do, you can enjoy them. Variation keeps you fresh mentally, but by the time we were in Argentina some of the players wanted to be rewarded although they weren't prepared to earn the rewards by doing the work.

My foot injury meant I wasn't in contention for the tests against the Australians in Sydney and Auckland in August. But watching the games on television it looked like an extension of the Argentinean tour. They just weren't performing, and the players seemed to have lost confidence. They lost in Sydney, 21-12, and then two weeks later scraped home, 6-3, at Eden Park. The Auckland win didn't really signal a return to form. The test would have been lost if Michael Lynagh had been in his usual kicking form.

John Hart had been heavily involved in the preparations for the Eden Park test. During the time before the World Cup squad was announced I talked a lot to Joe Stanley about how the Auckland guys were handling things. There were certainly plenty of Auckland players who were more than happy for Harty to be involved.

But then Eddie Tonks, the chairman of the New Zealand Rugby Union, insisted that Harty be co-coach at the World Cup.

It was ja recipe for failure, that could never work with two personalities as strong as Grizz and Harty. When it was first suggested, Grizz should have confronted Eddie Tonks and said, "Either I go as coach, or John Hart goes as coach. I won't go as co-coach." I talked with Joe Stanley about it, and it was his feeling that Harty shouldn't go. Joe and I knew that Harty would get his boys in behind him, some of Grizz's allies would stick with him, and the young guys would be left in midair, not knowing which way to jump. It would prove to be a problem even before the team left Auckland.

Hart and Wyllie were just so different as coaches, and as people. The last time they'd been together, to Japan, in 1986, they virtually didn't talk to each other. In blunt terms, Harty saw Grizz as a bumbling drunk, and Grizz saw Harty as a jumped-up little shit. It was the last thing you needed going into a World Cup.

Although I wasn't in the squad for the two Australian tests in the winter of '91, I spoke to Grizz Wyllie quite frequently. I was working at trying to get my foot right, and I told him, "If it comes right I'll tell you, but if it doesn't I'll be upfront and let you know."

As the time for the team to be announced got closer I reached a stage where I was able to tell him that for the first time since Argentina there were definite signs that the injury was coming right.

I said to Grizz, "I'll probably need two or three weeks on tour to get my general fitness back to what it should be, but I'd be right by quarter-final time."

He said, "That's good enough for me." When the World Cup squad was announced Gary was the captain and I was the vice-captain. There were apparently some rumours in the North Island that Alex asked me to be the captain, but they're not true.

* * *

Alex Wyllie: Mike is such a great team player that there was no doubt in my mind that when he said he was keen to be involved, he wouldn't have done that unless he was going to be fit enough to play. He would never put himself into a situation

47

where he might let the team down. He commands a lot of respect because of the soundness of his thinking, and as vice-captain I knew he'd do a marvellous job, especially with the guys who might not be playing. At a World Cup you've got to take some guys to cover positions, and they might not get a game. But they're important, and Mike was the sort of guy who would have kept them right up to the mark.

*   *   *

We assembled at the Poenamo Hotel in Takapuna, and John Sturgeon, the manager, Grizz, Harty, Gary and myself had a management meeting on the first morning. You could immediately feel the friction in the room, and we hadn't even had a training run.

I said, "Look, there's one thing I want to know, and the team should know. Who's the coach, and who is the assistant coach? As far as I'm concerned we need one coach, so the guys are directed by him, and then there's an assistant coach."

The room fell silent.

Then Harty, in his articulate way, took control.

"Well, the whole thing is Alex and I are going to bounce off each other the whole time. I'll be coming to Alex and he'll be coming to me with regard to player selection and game plans. We'll both be coming to you and Gary as well."

In the end I said, "I really don't think that's the right thing to happen. We've got to have one man in charge, and one man assisting."

I was told it'd be sorted out and they'd let the guys know. I don't believe that ever happened.

*   *   *

Alex Wyllie: What happened eventually was that on a Monday I'd take the forwards, and he (Hart) would take the backs. Then we'd get together and he'd run the whole team. On Tuesday it'd be my turn to take the whole team. It was a ridiculous situation, but I went along with it.

*   *   *

When a team assembles there's a shakedown period when various minor issues like rosters and rooming arrangements are worked out. Usually the medical is not much of a bigger deal than the other trivia.

I had been strapping my foot while I trained and played for Otago. I'd come on as a reserve against Taranaki in New Plymouth, then played against Canterbury and North Auckland at Carisbrook. Strapping the foot for the medical didn't seem likely to be a problem.

     *   *   *

Alex Wyllie: The whole test was basically a sham. Michael Jones strapped his knee, Zinzan Brooke strapped his ankles for every training run. If they'd been asked to take a fitness test unstrapped, they might have failed. Of course, they weren't.

     *   *   *

The examination was being run by a panel headed by Barry Tietjens, the Auckland orthopaedic surgeon. Dr John Mayhew, the All Black team doctor, was there, but he wasn't part of the medical advisory panel. Even before the exam I thought there was something a little strange going on.

Doc Mayhew came to me and said, "Mike, we want you to come and do your examination last."

That never happens. You just shoot across to Barry's offices. But Doc came to me specifically and asked me to leave it for another hour or so.

I asked Doc if I needed to strap my foot, but he said I didn't. I had a funny sort of feeling about it. I went to Barry's offices in Remuera Road, and we went through the basics of blood pressure and heart rate.

Then they asked me to take off my shoes, and from one foot do a standing jump up on to a chair, and down to the floor 10 times. I said, "I won't do that. The foot's at a stage now where it's coming right. If I was wearing an All Black jersey, I'd have my foot strapped. I'm not prepared to risk tearing it. I'll only do it if I can strap my foot."

They said, "No, you can't have a support."

So I said, "I won't do it then." That was when they pulled me out of the World Cup squad.

     *   *   *

John Mayhew: Players never wore strapping at examinations. It'd be like going to the dentist wearing a mouthguard. Obviously we would have taken into account if a guy had an injury, but he could play with strapping within 10 days. That was the criteria then. It's been reviewed and changed subsequent to the Robin Brooke fiasco in 1993 (when Brooke left New Zealand with a calf muscle injury and was unable to play at all on tour). None of the doctors involved on the panel, or myself, were under any special instructions from anybody on the New Zealand Rugby Union. We examined Mike like we examined the others. No knee brace, no strapping, nothing like that. He was asked to stand on one foot and jump off the ground. He wasn't willing to try that. When the medical decision was made I communicated that to Harty and Grizz at the Poe, and they still wanted to take him on tour, to overturn the decision. Sturgy (John Sturgeon, the All Blacks manager) felt that was wrong, and the final decision, as I understand it, was made by Eddie Tonks.

*   *   *

Alex Wyllie: Sturge came to me and said, "Mike Brewer's out." I said, "Bullshit." I rang Eddie Tonks and he said, "I know how you feel, but if the medical guys say he's not fit, and he breaks down, how silly will we look?" It still amazes me. We (the All Black management group) had been going to all the medicals for a couple of years. Then someone said we didn't have to go this time. The way we'd picked the team, if there was some doubt about Mike we only needed him for a couple of games late in the Cup to cover for Michael Jones. If his injury was a wee bit suspect early on, we knew he could play in those games.

*   *   *

John Mayhew: It was never communicated to us (the medical team) that they were prepared to not have Mike play until the quarter-finals. Grizz has a lot of good points, but he never gave us much guidance on that sort of thing. I'm not slagging Grizz. Harty didn't explain that to us either. The decision was made on the basis that he had to be available to play all six World Cup games. I didn't make the decision, but I fully agreed with it.

Grizz and Harty wanted the panel's decision overturned. To

me, that would have made a nonsense of having a medical examination. If the advice of the medical advisory committee wasn't going to be taken, why bother having it? In the end they rang Eddie Tonks, and he made the final decision. Subsequently Mike played a couple of games for Otago, and played very well, but that was a different scenario from playing in a World Cup and training every day.

*   *   *

Colin Calcinai: I am the chairman of the New Zealand Rugby Union's medical advisory committee, and in that role I supervised the panel that examined the World Cup squad in 1991. It was a very experienced group. As well as Barry Tietjens we had Peter Cuningham, who had previously been an All Black doctor on tour, and Tony Edwards and Ian Rapson, who are medical officers with the New Zealand Olympic and Commonwealth Games Association. We had no special instructions for Mike's examination, beyond the general instruction from the NZRFU, that players should be fit to play within a week or 10 days of leaving the country. Naturally we were all aware of Mike's history with his plantar fascia rupture. He was examined clinically, and put through a range of movement. It was a very severe injury. He couldn't stand on his toes with the foot unstrapped. I make no apologies for the decision to recommend that he would not be able to withstand the rigours of a World Cup campaign. It was a unanimous decision by the entire panel. We did ask Mike to jump and and down off a stool, but his refusal was not the basis of our decision. It was part of it, but really a very small part of the assessment. The nature of the injury was such that we could see no useful or reliable repair for it. It was a very rare injury that nobody had a lot of experience with, and in any medical examination, nothing can be guaranteed to be 100 per cent foolproof. But we had to make a decision, and we are obliged to be honest in our assessment to the NZRFU. In our opinion he would not have withstood the rigours of the World Cup.

*   *   *

When the panel said that I might not last through the World Cup, with training every day, I couldn't say that they were right

51

or wrong. But really, what I believe it should have come down to was that Alex, who I saw as the coach, wanted to take the risk, and he should have been allowed to decide. I still think it should be the coach's prerogative.

The one thing that pissed me off the most was that after I'd failed the medical, Harty asked me to stay in Auckland and play for the Barbarians against the All Blacks, in the training match they had before they flew out. Grizz had some clear advice on that. "Tell them to get f***ed." I think I just said to Harty, "No thanks, I'll go back and train with the Otago team. I might get a run with them."

As it happened, Laurie Mains had already picked the team to play Wellington, so I was on the bench. The boys were playing so badly that with about 20 minutes to go Laurie sent word out to Arran Pene that he was coming off. When I ran out I've never had a reception like it at any provincial park in New Zealand. There was just about a standing ovation. Then I got the ball on the 22, and ran in what proved to be the winning try. Keith Quinn was doing the commentary, and was calling me "the man they say isn't fit enough to play the World Cup."

In the end it was a good provincial season for me. Otago won the national championship, and then the BP company organised a trip, and shouted Bev and I. We finally caught up with the All Blacks in Dublin. Joe Stanley was leading another tour group, and we ran into Michael Jones not long before the semifinal. The Iceman was just about pleading with Joe and I to come in and see the team. He wanted us to stay with the team right then.

Michael was really distressed. He said the World Cup had been terrible and there were two groups, with the team just split in half. We saw Paul Henderson, and he said to me, "Would you like to swap places? This is the worst tour I've ever been on."

*   *   *

Alex Wyllie: We lost the unifying spirit at the World Cup. You'd see Hart going off with six or seven players, all of them from Auckland. I'd seem them walking out of the hotel. I mean, shit, it was exactly what I thought was going to happen.

*   *   *

Paul Henderson: There was just no rhyme or reason to the whole exercise. We had Hart and Wyllie at each others' throats, and from my point of view having three openside flankers at the World Cup was ridiculous. You need match play. It was just a strange situation. There was no common goal with everyone, so it just led to disappointment all over. I get on fine with Gary Whetton, I like him, but he wouldn't even stretch with us. I remember very clearly the rest of us down on one knee, stretching our hamstrings, and GeeDub just standing there with his arms folded. He was at that stage in his career where he just couldn't be bothered with it. Those were the sort of things that were symptoms of what was happening throughout the squad. I would have wanted to be there just to load the bags really, but it was very disappointing that we didn't give the thing 100 per cent.

*   *   *

Seven or eight minutes into the semifinal in Dublin I turned to Bev, and said, "There's no way we're going to win this. There's no attitude, no desire to succeed." To me it was the culmination of a lot of things. The "plague of selfishness", which led to such individuality, and the training not being hard enough, which led to the lack of fitness.

I felt even worse watching the playoff for third and fourth in Cardiff. I was that wild I felt that some of the players didn't deserve to be wearing the black jersey. Afterwards we were invited to the Crest Hotel to be with the team. Bev wouldn't let me go. She knew what sort of mood I was in.

4

Welcome Aboard

Not long after Laurie Mains was appointed to coach the All Blacks he told me that Gary Whetton was out of the picture, and he wanted me to captain the side.

It may sound odd, but I had never had any inclination to captain the All Blacks. I would have jumped at the job if all that had been involved was the training and the playing.

But the off field requirements just take up so much time, and that was the part that I wasn't keen on. I love the game of rugby for the sport that it is, what it's given me and the joy it's brought to my family as well.

I also like a private life, and the only thing I don't like about being an All Black is not being able to go unnoticed. When you're the captain of the All Blacks that's even more pronounced.

However, I was quite happy to captain the team if Laurie wanted me to. He became coach very shortly after the World Cup in Britain, where the attitude of the All Blacks had disillusioned me so much, and knowing him so well, I was sure he'd bring back some discipline and pride into the team.

Laurie would give total loyalty and commitment to the team, as he'd shown even when coaching his club side, Southern. He battled to be allowed to play his rep players when they were wanted by the Otago coach, Lee Smith. When Laurie became the Otago coach he even got me to shoot back after the Baby

Blacks test in Christchurch to play for Otago on the Sunday.

I knew with the national team he'd put even more emphasis on rugby, already a huge part of his life, to make sure they succeeded. So although he wasn't perceived in a positive light by the northern media in particular, I was very much looking forward to working with Laurie.

*　　*　　*

Laurie Mains: There's no secret about the fact I wanted Mike to be my All Black captain. Putting aside the respect I had for him as a player and captain, a very important factor was that he understood me, which was going to make him a very good liaison in getting my philosophies across to the players. He had a directness, and the ability to be up front on team issues, and to present them to me. That was very important. But the most important aspect was his ability to read a game, and to play the tactics that are required. Loose forward is an ideal position for a captain. So it was going to make it a much smoother transition if he was there. I talked with him about it after I was appointed, but we didn't spend hours on the phone talking about this player or that. And let's make one thing clear: At no stage after I was appointed coach did Mike seek the captaincy. He would have done it if he'd been required. That's his very matter of fact approach to the whole thing. Gary Whetton? We knew we were going to be turning some people over, and the obvious ones to go first were those we had some real doubts over whether they'd be 100 per cent with us. If Gary had been in the team he wouldn't have been the captain, and my guess is he would have had some real difficulty playing under Mike.

*　　*　　*

In the second week in April in '92 they had a week of trials. In the Saturday trial Steve McDowell captained one team, and I captained the other. Two minutes into the second half I blew a calf muscle. The first of the New Zealand Rugby Union centenary matches was a week away, so I was out of contention.

Sean Fitzpatrick became the obvious candidate for captaincy. It probably came down to him and Grant Fox. But at that stage the selectors were talking about a different style of backline play, and there was a chance Foxy might not be in the team. Sean was appointed captain.

*　　*　　*

Laurie Mains: It took a little while for me to understand Sean, but having got through the centennial games with him, I decided to stay with him for the Irish tests, and the tour to Australia and South Africa. The first guy I rang when I'd made the decision to stay with Sean was Mike. He had no difficulty with it at all. I don't believe it concerned him one iota, one jot, that I'd decided to stay with Sean. There were two reasons for deciding to continue with Sean. One was that I like his style. He's straight up and down as well. The other was that I had reliability there. I could pretty much guarantee with Sean that he was going to be there for every test match. Whereas with Mike, to bring him back on the off chance he might get through the rest of the season, and then perhaps have him injured again, and have to bring Sean in again, wouldn't be good for the whole of the team. It was something I respected so much about Mike. He was happy to take the lesser role. I guess it comes back to the inner confidence and security, and the fact he doesn't have an ego. What you see is what you get. It's refreshing and I found that hell of a good to work with.

*　　*　　*

When I've been playing in the team alongside Sean we work together. I'm sure he's aware of rather malicious suggestions that at times the captain's decisions on the field are being made by me, rather than him.

But the good thing is that we really do have a partnership. I'd suggest we're two of the players in the All Blacks with egos that don't need stroking. With our relationship, how we approach the game, and our passion for the All Blacks to succeed, it works well. Sean knows I totally support him as a captain, and don't want his captaincy. He does a fine job.

The first time I can remember us meeting each other was at the trials for the Baby Blacks, and even when we were in the All Blacks together in the 80s, I can't recall mixing with him too much socially. Naturally enough he was closer to his Auckland teammates, Gary and AJ Whetton and Foxy. He stayed pretty quiet, sitting in the wings and absorbing things.

That was off the field. On the field he made a much greater impression. Playing against him when he was in Auckland colours he was fiercely competitive, not giving an inch, to the stage where he was probably one of the most physical players in the country. He knew how to play it very hard, without getting caught.

There are some people who didn't take to the way Sean was very vocal on the field, but that's never concerned me at all. I don't have a problem, at the top level, with a player who is getting on top of his opponent physically, hammering the point home verbally.

I've done it myself. In the Canterbury challenge for the Ranfurly Shield in Hamilton, Tom Coventry came on as a replacement flanker. I was winning a bit of ball by then, and was totally confident in the throwing of Matt Sexton.

Tom was beside me in the lineout, and it was our throw. I said to him, "This one's coming to you, Tommy, let's see how good you are." I called the throw to myself, got it, and we ended up with Simon Forrest scoring a try.

I ran up beside Tom, and said to him, "You're still not good enough, Tommy." If a player takes it to heart, in a negative way, you have a big advantage established over him for the rest of the game, and possibly every time you play.

Some of our best players have been champion sledgers. The great Colin Meads once told me that if he was beaten in the first lineout of a test by his marker, he'd snarl at the guy, "Do that again, and I'll kill you!" In most cases Pinetree would get the ball for the rest of the game. And Fitzy and John Kirwan certainly let their markers know if they were getting the upper hand.

In 1992 when Auckland played Ireland, and beat them 62-7, the Irish had such a long injury list going into the game, that JK was marking Neville Furlong, who had a bad foot injury.

The first time Furlong tried to tackle JK he fended him off, scored a try, and said, "Too soft, arsehole."

The Irishman just gritted his teeth. The next time JK got the ball Furlong hit him with a hard tackle, but JK got the ball away, and another Aucklander scored.

"Too slow, arsehole" said JK.

Play went on, and again JK handed him off, got another try, and said, "Not up to it, arsehole."

Late in the game Ireland managed to get an overlap near the line, and Furlong, his aching ankle now bandaged like a mummy, was the man who went across for the try.

JK still wasn't lost for words.

"Soft try, arsehole," he murmured to Furlong.

"And you," shot back Furlong, "couldn't stop a f**kin' cripple, arsehole!"

Sean brings real passion to New Zealand rugby. With the front row the first point of confrontation you must have a trio who dominate. That sets things alight for the rest of the tight five, your loosies, then your backs.

In 1987 he made up what I believe was the best front row New Zealand has ever had, with Steve McDowell and John Drake. John was enormously under-rated as a tighthead prop, except by the people who played with, or against, him. Those three could dominate a scrum, and steamroll over almost everyone they packed down against.

In fact, every scrum Sean seems to be in goes well, no matter who the props are. It must be his size and strength and skill that has something to do with that. And because of his competitiveness he hates going back in any scrum. Any scrum he hits, he wants to be in charge.

Early in his career, if he had any weakness, it was throwing in to the lineout. In '86 he wasn't consistent, but he's worked a hell of a lot on his throwing over the years. A lineout jumper is only as good as the guy throwing the ball in, so it's an art a hooker has to perfect. That's exactly what Sean has done.

After missing the games against the World XV in '92 because of my calf injury, I was back in the All Blacks for the games against Ireland, and then for the tour to Australia and South Africa.

Laurie, Sean and I sat down and had a chat, knowing that we all had to work together. Sean said, "I need your help for some on the field direction, and key decision making. I've got my head down in the hard stuff, and I need some eyes in the open."

That's the way we've basically worked since, when I've been in the team. It's a partnership. There's nothing unusual about it. The fact is that hooker is a difficult position from which to captain a team. Any captain who is a hooker has to rely on other players in the team to shoulder some responsibility. Input that's solicited doesn't undermine the captain's authority at all. I learned that when I was captaining Otago.

When there's a break in play Sean gets the team together, and if he has to, revs them up. For some option taking it revolves around the loose forward trio, usually myself and Zinzan Brooke, and the inside backs.

Until Foxy retired it was relatively easy. Foxy had the confidence to call the shots. It was harder when Stephen Bachop came on board, because he wasn't so confident. So it often came down to Zinny or myself to make the tactical decisions.

In '93 Laurie gave the responsibility for the lineout calls to Arran Pene, and in '94 to me. Basically I want the ball thrown to where it's being won. For that reason in '94 nine out of ten throws were directed to Ian Jones.

Some players, or captains, think all the jumpers should get an even share of the throws, but my opinion is that you throw to the same guy all day if he can win it.

*   *   *

Laurie Mains: Mike is absolutely delighted to be selected to play in an All Black team. Every time his name is read out he's over the moon. The captaincy is not an issue. There's no difficulty between Mike and Sean because they know their respective roles. He's not cutting across Sean's bows, it's just not practical for a tight forward to tactically lead a team at all times. It doesn't matter who your captain is, there are lieutenants within the team who have to make decisions. People who understand rugby would know that. Mike is remarkably restrained at times, so that he's not seen by the other players to be horning in on Sean's territory. In the heat of a game Mike may get a little bit dominant, but that's because of his absolute commitment. He'll be demanding of the players immediately around him, the halfback, the first five, but he won't cut across the pattern as laid down by Sean. To me it's a mark of Sean's self esteem and security that he feels comfortable about Mike giving him a hand. Look, these top test players that have gone through the mill, and come out of it as men, they know it's too big for egos to wreck it.

*   *   *

My tour to Australia was cut short after the first test, which we lost in Sydney by just one point. I was tackled heavily on to my shoulder, damaged the AC joint, and was out for almost six weeks, which meant missing not only the rest of the Australian tour, but the ground breaking visit to South Africa.

Times were changing in the All Blacks with Laurie as coach. While I didn't think some of the training runs we had in Australia were as tough as some of the runs in the old days in Otago, Laurie did get us back to the idea of training harder than you have to play.

In rugby you have to get your heart rate up, and hold it for a long time. To do that you sometimes have to bust a gut in training. Laurie has a petty basic philosophy with back play now, and that is that you need continuity to beat opposing defences.

That means you must have forwards getting to breakdowns, but also backs who can back up, quickly get back into position, and back up again.

Now a back might be the fastest player in the team in a straight sprint, but if he doesn't have the aerobic base to keep up the work rate, after 10 minutes he's going to be tired, and that speed won't be available when it's needed.

It took some of the players a while to fully believe in the way Laurie ran the team, but someone like Zinzan Brooke became a believer in '92 as the intensive work got him fitter and fitter, and he eventually produced some of the best form of his All Black career.

Just one unfortunate element had crept into the team in '92, and that was an "us and them" feeling that grew up in the players who usually found themselves in the midweek side.

On my first tour with the All Blacks I'd been deeply impressed with the way Cowboy Shaw had urged the midweek team to train harder and harder, to put pressure on the players in the Saturday side. Then, after winning the midweek games, they'd get right in and support if they didn't make the Saturday side.

A wee bit of jealousy crept into the midweekers in '92, and it was disappointing to see the attitude of Terry Wright. He thought he should have been in the Saturday team, but the coach and management didn't think so.

Instead of taking it on the chin, and, as a senior player, encouraging the midweek players to get stuck in, he packed a sad on the matter, taking the attitude the management weren't interested in the midweekers. It almost divided the team.

Of course management and the weekend team are interested in the midweekers. There's nothing worse on tour than watching an All Black side lose, any All Black side, whether it's on a Wednesday or a Saturday. The team is the team.

Having played out the '92 season with Otago, I had no intention of playing any football in 1993, in Canterbury, not even club play. My reasoning was that there was no point in turning out for a club if you weren't fully fit, and if you were fully fit for club rugby, you might as well be available for higher levels too.

Eventually I did play for Canterbury, right at the end of the season, and, because I was hoping to play again in '94, when I went to Britain at the end of '93 as a liaison man with the All Blacks for Canterbury International. I was happy to train with the All Blacks when the offer was made. I still had no intention of playing for them.

*   *   *

Laurie Mains: On the Thursday before the test against England I could see a difficult situation arising for us. Paul Henderson had a calf muscle that had failed to come right for a couple of weeks. Zinny hurt his ankle at the Thursday training, too, so we talked through the options. Sean raised it with me.

"What will you do about a reserve?"

We knew it was possible, if not probable, that Zinny might not get through the game. We looked at what we had, and we needed a bit of pace, and also the size and physical strength of

Rodber, Richards and Clarke. We were starting the game with Arran Pene at No 8, Zinny at openside and Jamie Joseph at blindside flanker.

It was obvious that Jamie or Arran could never in your wildest dreams be played off the back of the lineout. We discussed the players we had in the squad and it was agreed that we really didn't have one with both the pace, and the size, to fit the bill.

Then Sean said to me, "What about Bruiser?"

We kicked it around a bit, and Mike had been training at times with the team on tour. So for the straight out good of the team, looking at what was going to give us our best cover for the test match, none of us could argue against the idea of calling on Mike.

But I also knew it might be difficult, and look as if we weren't doing the right thing. I hoped like hell that Paul Henderson would come right. I talked the situation through with our manager, Neil Gray, and we agreed we'd keep the plan under wraps.

I took the liberty of ringing Mike and saying, "Where are you going to be between noon and one tomorrow? I may want to talk to you about something." No clues as to what it was about. He said I'd get him at the hotel. I said, "Make sure you're there between twelve and one."

On the Friday we went to Twickenham, and I said to Ric Salizzo (the All Blacks media liaison man) to come with us. He had no idea what was going on. I said to Ric, "We may have a difficult PR situation to deal with."

But when we were dropping off the dirt trackers (the non-test squad) at their training, Neil said he wanted Ric to stay with them. They were going on to a promotion after they'd trained. I said to Neil, "I think Ric should stay with us in case we need to get Bruiser in." But Neil said, "I'll deal with it." I said, "Really, it's Ric's thing," but Neil insisted he'd deal with it.

We got to Twickenham and Ginge (Henderson) started doing his training. I asked how he was, and he said he wouldn't know until he warmed up. After 10 minutes he came to me and said, "I've got to pull out."

Fortunately, just before the training, I saw Eddie Tonks (the chairman of the New Zealand Rugby Union) arrive. He was leaning on the fence chatting to Neil. I called Sean over and said, "Eddie Tonks is over there, let's go and talk about this Bruiser thing."

So we went into the changing room. There was Neil Gray, Eddie Tonks, Sean and myself. Earle Kirton (the assistant coach) was with the dirt trackers. We outlined the plan to Eddie. He said, "I'm not totally comfortable with it, but if that's what you want to do, I'll go along with it. The final decision is the manager's."

So Eddie, as chairman, had been given the chance to veto the idea. He said he wasn't totally comfortable with it, but that he'd okay it if the manager was happy.

After the tour Neil Gray would say that he hadn't wanted Mike to be included in the reserves for the test. But at the time Neil told us he was comfortable with it. In fact, when I rang Mike to tell him what I wanted him to do he said, "I knew about it last night. I was at a dinner with Neil, and he told me." I didn't make an issue of it at the time, but does that sound as if Neil was a man opposed to the idea?

When we were in England we had no idea of the controversy that was building back home. We looked at where we were in the tour, and the fact that Matthew Cooper was ruled out of the rest of the games through injury. Mike replaced Matthew as an official member of the touring party, which as far as we were concerned made us quite entitled to play him in the last two games.

But I told Mike we would only use him as a reserve, because there were players who had been on the whole tour. In the midweek game between the England test and the Barbarians match we played Ginge (with John Mitchell at No 8, and Liam Barry at blindside flanker), and Ginge got through the game. But the next day Ginge couldn't even train, and he said, "That's it for me."

We ruled Jamie Joseph out of the Barbarians game (after a stomping incident in the England test) and we went with Mike, as a reserve, because he could cover both blindside and openside for us. We weren't going to start him in the match, but when he came on as a replacement for Blair Larsen, that apparently sparked a lot of the antagonistic feeling back in New Zealand.

*   *   *

Editorial, *1994 Rugby Almanack*: The introduction of Mike Brewer to the reserves for the England international ahead of Liam Barry and John Mitchell, two fit loose forwards who were members of the touring party, was an insult to these players, and one of the worst selection decisions in All Black history. We have not spoken to one rugby follower who approved of the management's decision.

*   *   *

Laurie Mains: When we got back home Neil Gray and I were left to carry the can for the decision over Mike. Eddie Tonks was fully involved in the decision, and I doubt whether the public of New Zealand would know that.

It had been a long, hard season in 1993, and I recognised that I might not be reading the decision right. So the opportunity was given to the chairman of the union to make a rational decision and he made one. When it turned to trouble there was a lack of support from Eddie. Neil Gray bailed it on to us when there was strong anti-comment too.

*   *   *

I was at a Wasps club dinner in London with some of the guys from Canterbury International when Neil Gray came up to me.

He said, "You'd better go easy on the wine tonight."

I asked him what he meant. It wasn't as if I had a game coming up.

"You might," Neil replied. "Ginge is doubtful for Saturday, and he's got a fitness test tomorrow morning." Neil said the management and Sean had discussed it, and might want me to stand by as a reserve.

He assured me that the whole issue had been talked through, and agreed to, by everyone from Eddie Tonks to the players. Next day I was almost out the door of the hotel when the phone range. Ginge was out of contention, and I moved from my hotel in London to Bagshot where the team was staying.

I'd caught up with the guys initially at the third match of the tour in Redruth, and from then on I'd probably been at 75 per

64

In my scarfie days in Dunedin, wearing the Cambridge blue jersey of the University club. Brewer family collection

Eric Champ shows some unusual skills as we contest the ball at Nantes in 1986, a test where I have never seen such glassy-eyed opponents. Peter Bush

Before the trials in 1986 I'd never heard of Brent Harvey, the Wairarapa-Bush flanker, but he was the man who inpassed to me for my first, and only, test try, for the Baby Blacks against France at Lancaster Park.   Brewer family collection

Contesting the ball against the French in my first test in 1986. In the first half I felt tired, which worried me because I thought we'd only been playing for 10 minutes. I looked at the clock . . . it was only two minutes to halftime.

Brewer family collection

Mark "Cowboy" Shaw, a huge influence on my first All Black tour in 1986 and I pinning down the lineout ball against a Cote de Basque XV. Ross Setford, Fotopacific

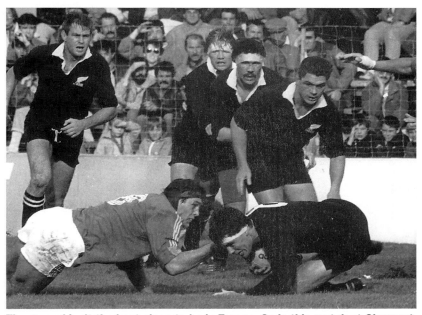

The ground isn't the best place to be in France. So in this match at Clermont-Ferrand in 1986 it's probably for the best that support is at hand from **Mark Shaw, Michael Speight, Murray Pierce and Mark Brooke-Cowden.** Peter Bush

Tourist time in Japan as Gary Whetton and I feed tame deer at Nara Park.

Peter Bush

Why is this man laughing? He's just worked out the price of these melons in a Tokyo supermarket in 1987, and they're between $NZ80 and $NZ100 each.

Peter Bush

One peak of the golden era in the late '80s for the All Blacks was the 1988 tour of Australia. In the first test at Sydney I'm looking for space and seem to have a handy break on Wallaby flyhalf Michael Lynagh. Peter Bush

cent of training sessions, right through England and Scotland. So as far as training, knowing what was going on, knowing the pattern of play and the calls, there wasn't a problem. I was still a bit apprehensive, but having done the training I was prepared to do the job they asked me to do.

After the England test I joined the team officially, and when it came to selecting the team and reserves for the Barbarians game, they had even more pressure on them with Jamie being stood down. When you're on tour you view the Barbarians game as another test, and nothing had changed with the '93 team. In hindsight I don't think the decision to make me a reserve was any different from the England test.

Some people read something sinister into Sean shaking hands with me when I came on as a replacement, for an injured Blair Larsen, late in the Barbarians game. There was actually nothing more to it than a "welcome aboard." Sean and I played our first test together, in '86, and like many players you've shared a lot with, when you get selected for another test, you shake hands. The Barbarians' match was my first, and only, game of the tour, and it didn't seem strange to me that there was a handshake.

But once we were back home the conspiracy theories started flying, and one of the wilder ones was that the handshake was almost a secret society gesture, a nod and a wink between Sean and myself that I would share in the All Blacks Ltd payout at the end of the year.

That's nonsense, but I did take a share, just over $4000 to be precise, when the dividends from promotional payments were issued. Why? Because I knew that not just the letter, but the spirit, of the agreements worked out by a players' committee very definitely entitled a replacement to some recompense, even if he was literally on the field for 30 seconds.

How did I know? Because, along with John Kirwan and Gary Whetton, I was one of the players who had worked with officials to set up the guidelines and rules for payments from All Blacks Ltd, which is now largely superceded by the All Blacks Club.

We (the players' committee members) didn't want a situation where a player in a home series, for example, could spend five tests on the bench, with all the time and effort involved in that, play briefly in just one test, and be left entirely empty-handed.

The player contracts have all changed now, but in '93 I felt it was important to stick with what we'd agreed. Then, in the future, pressure wouldn't go on a player to turn down what, when we set up the system, we believed he deserved. And personally I felt that over the years I'd devoted enough time to the All Blacks, as a player, and as a players' representative, racing up and down to Wellington, to quite fairly take what was offered. I still believe that was a reasonable attitude.

5

Winter of Discontent

It never looked likely to be a happy winter for the All Blacks in
1994. For a start, none of the players were keen about the idea
of playing six tests in eight weeks, finishing with a Bledisloe Cup
test under lights in Sydney just 10 days after the Springbok series
finished.

I also had the feeling that the players hadn't prepared
themselves well, and when players know they're going to be
struggling to last the distance, they lose confidence in themselves.

You could tell at training that players were holding back. They
weren't firing into it, giving 110 per cent from the start. In the
past, we'd trained flat out from the beginning of a session, but
now if we were playing touch, or going through some skills, guys
would just be cruising, in case the training was longer than they
expected. They weren't sure they'd get through it. I remember
talking to Laurie about it during the season.

In 1992 he could introduce himself to the team, and say, "This
is what I'm capable of." The players were never sure what they
were going to get. They might be doing 15 strideouts of 120
metres, then a set of down and ups, and then the scrum-ruck
machine, all in one training run. If you do get that you go back
to the hotel, flag lunch, and just lie on your bed for an hour. But
once you're used to it, it's of immense value when it comes to the
game. He probably had to loosen the reins a bit, because if he'd

really hammered them through '93 and '94, it would have been too much when you came to put the hammer down in '95.

*   *   *

Laurie Mains: When we gave out our official training programmes before the winters of '92 and '93 we enforced them. We didn't do that before the winter of '94. We had to accept the fact the players were amateurs, and if we put the screws on too hard over those three summers, what would we have left for 1995? Mike's been a bit critical that the guys weren't fit enough in '94, but the whole philosophy was that if we made it voluntary in '94, then when we came to '95 we could say, "Right this is not an option. Either you do the training we want you to do, or you're not in the team. This is a compulsory commitment."

*   *   *

In the '93-94 summer I didn't get a programme from the All Blacks, so I basically did a mixture of running to build back some aerobic fitness. There were some runs of up to 12km on the roads and through bush, and some 400 and 800 metres on grass tracks. I really only did about a week of speed work before the first trial in Gisborne. My aim was to try to peak at about the time of the second test in Wellington against the Springboks.

The first trial in Gisborne saw two evenly matched teams on paper, but the side I was in had older footballers, who possibly knew the benefits of aerobic training over summer. The opposition got away on us a bit, but we clawed back, and in the end won quite comfortably. Our forwards were much faster to the loose ball as fitness started to count. I was personally very happy with how the trial went.

In Napier the second trial was very fast, with some great matchups, such as Jonah Lomu against John Kirwan. Again, in the second half our forwards got some dominance, and we won.

Our first test of the season was against France, at Lancaster Park, on a Sunday. Pierre Berbizier, their coach, had obviously looked hard at the way we'd been playing and devised a plan to beat us.

They stood up tight in the midfield, and didn't commit themselves in the rucks and mauls, so there were forwards available to knock our runners and our midfield over.

We seemed to go into the test in the belief that their first and second fives were poor tacklers. I watched the New Zealand XV play France the weekend before the test, and said to Laurie that I believed the first five, Christophe Deylaud, was actually not a bad tackler at all. He made his tackles, and so did the men outside him, Thierry Lacroix and Philippe Sella.

While the All Blacks had power in the midfield, and on the wing with Jonah Lomu, we didn't have good passers, and we couldn't get the ball wide. In the end we were trying to bust through the midfield, but from static ball, and we got knocked over all day. We couldn't get over the advantage line and get a roll on.

In fact, the Christchurch test was the only time in '94 when I actually felt some tinges of panic during a game. If we moved it to the backs we ended up going backwards to the breakdown. If we kicked, we kicked to the wrong place, and the French would counter attack and make more yards We couldn't get a drive on from the lineout, and the scrums didn't go that well. To be really blunt, no matter what we did that day it turned to shit.

With 20 minutes to go you knew that all you could do was try to stay in the game, and not let the score get away too much. You knew you couldn't win it. In Auckland, in the second test, the French soaked up the pressure, and stayed composed, even when we were dominating the game. With just three minutes to go they got what was really only their second scoring chance in the game. Philippe Saint-Andre counter attacked from inside his own 22, and after seven other payers had handled without error, Jean-Luc Sadourny scored the match winning try. It was hard to accept, but that's test rugby.

By the time the second test was over, the All Blacks were under what was virtually a media siege. Everyone from Paul Holmes to Murray Deaker was calling for Laurie's sacking, and, as individuals, we were being rubbished relentlessly.

Our manager, Colin Meads, had the theory that with our politicians mainly disliked, and no war heroes, New Zealand's sportspeople have become the ones people look to. That's fine when teams are winning, but, as the All Blacks found in '94, and the New Zealand cricket team found the following summer, when the teams are losing there's a real price to pay.

Harsh feedback from the public and the media can eat away at player confidence, but it's a chicken and the egg situation. If you prepare yourself as a player both mentally and physically, and the coaches are well prepared, with their plan worked out, then you end up playing well, and you don't get that backlash from the press and the public.

Constructive criticism is very important in sport, especially in team sports, and in the case of the All Blacks, it nearly always spurs them on. They might hate hearing it at the time, but it does act as a spur.

We had problems in '94 because we struggled to establish a style of play. We wanted to move the ball wide against the French, but our backline didn't function smoothly enough to do so.

I felt at times we were reactive, which was partly the result of stress. As you head towards a World Cup, to get the best out of players and a coach you need to know you have a coaching staff that has been appointed from one World Cup through to the next. In 1994 there was never that security for Laurie and the selection panel.

*   *   *

Laurie Mains: I'd asked, through the chairman (Eddie Tonks), that at the end of 1993 the New Zealand council make a decision on who would be the coach for the World Cup. If a new guy was going to come in he needed the '94 season to get the team sorted. Whoever was going to take the team to the World Cup should have known 18 months out. I asked for that in late '93, but I don't know if it was ever presented to the council for a vote by the chairman. It left the door open for anybody looking for controversy from the media to walk right in and ferment controversies. And there were plenty of people north of the Bombay Hills quite prepared to fuel the fire.

*   *   *

If a coach and selectors had been appointed right through to the Cup, they would know where they stood, know what style of play they wanted to use to win the Cup, and they could start tagging players from when they were in the Colts.

Knowing who they wanted to play that style they could begin to sit down and talk with players, and give them confidence to play their game. They could let players know that barring injury or loss of form, they were the ones for the World Cup.

That would lead to more consistency of selection, and you could also create an environment where you know you might have to drop some game along the way. That's where building up a good relationship with the media is important.

Then you can say, "This is what we're trying to do now, to create this result at the end." If they decide to play Marc Ellis at hooker, then when the media see Marc throwing the ball into the first lineout they don't bag him so much. They know the underlying thought is to have him there for the World Cup.

But to create that type of trust and understanding, it must flow down from the top, from the administration, to the coaches, to the players.

In '94 the selection panel was in an invidious position. They didn't know if they were going to be there for the World Cup themselves. The All Blacks had to keep on winning, or there could have been a major upheaval on the verge of the '95 Cup. The worst thing was, it was a problem of our own making, coming out of a boardroom in Wellington.

Changes were forced on the panel by a need for new inside backs, and by the need for a consistent goalkicker. In other circumstances there might have been time to persist with some players for longer, and the effect of the pressure was that some of the backs were going on to the park knowing that they didn't want to make mistakes. Instead of playing the game they were picked for, they ended up just shovelling the ball on, because they didn't want to commit an error.

In fact, backs need to have the confidence to believe that every time they get the ball, they can beat their opponents one on one. If they end up in fact getting tackled, then, "bang", the forwards are there to support them.

Really, that was the crux of the great era of 1987-90. It wasn't a matter of great genius, working out complicated ways to beat the opposition. It was winning quality ball on the front foot, and then moving the ball around. Backs could beat an opponent with footwork, or with passing skills, like Joe Stanley. If that didn't come up, you had a loose forward trio who arrived one, pause, two, pause, three. Then the tighties arrived as one straight afterwards.

*   *   *

Laurie Mains: At the start of the year we had Inga Tuigamala to replace, and that was a worry for us, because we made so much play off him.

Then we had a first-five in Marc Ellis who, apart from one game, we felt came on tremendously well on the tour to Britain in 1993. When we selected him for Britain, we said, "If he goes okay in Britain, what other rugby can we guarantee him at first-five before the World Cup?" At the start of '94 there was a seven match tour to Argentina, three games for New Zealand Universities, and two All Black trials. So there were 10 games, at least, plus games at first-five for his club. Gordon Hunter, the Otago coach, told us he'd play Ellis at first-five, not in crucial games, but in others.

Then we had a real concern about Stephen Bachop's tackling. When Michael Jones was playing you had a lot less concern about the first-five's tackling because he has this absolutely uncanny knack of being in exactly the right place to see what's developing, and to be there to make the pressure tackles.

But we knew we wouldn't have Michael against France, with the Sunday tests, and it was debatable whether he'd be there after that. We had some real problems with Stephen Bachop, in that under pressure in Britain he had shown some deficiencies.

Now Simon Mannix had played extremely well in both the Gisborne and Napier trials in '94, and had done so in the main All Black trial in Pukekohe the previous year. But trials can deceive you. Simon Mannix was not really able to handle test football.

When it came to replacing Inga, I don't think too many people would have said before the French tests that we made an error of judgement in picking Jonah Lomu. Where we made an error was in not fully realising that because our backline wasn't a stable unit because of injury, putting a kid like Jonah who had only played a handful of games on the wing for his province into a test was a risk we shouldn't have taken.

What capped it off was that Matthew Cooper was just out of sorts. If Matthew had been fully over his injury, and playing as well at second-five as he did in Britain, we'd have got away with it. But one mistake compounded the other.

*   *   *

So we had some players who deep down had doubts over their fitness levels, and then, when there wasn't selection consistency, the individuals concerned started to really struggle. The selectors needed to win the tests to secure their positions, and when they aren't won, lines start automatically going through some players' names.

Against South Africa it was really only in the second test in Wellington that we played what was a really good standard of rugby. After winning the first test in Dunedin, a lot had been made of the fact that the All Blacks always seem to lose the second test against South Africa, and they always seem to lose it in Wellington.

Somehow, despite winning the first test, we managed to go into the second test as underdogs. But we knew we had a far stronger forward pack than the Africans, and that if we really confronted them we could blow them to bits in the set pieces, and with the ball in hand.

That was the way we approached that second test, and we managed to get a game, considering the weather, of some continuity going. Although the final score was close, at 13-9, we actually dominated the whole game.

As it happened, the test will probably be remembered by most people, not for the fact that the All Blacks got their act together, but for Johan Le Roux biting Sean Fitzpatrick's ear.

Before the Springboks had arrived we'd looked at videos of the South Africans playing England, and it was obvious that Le Roux spent most of the game running round the field being a thug, trying to maim people.

Sure enough, in the first test in Dunedin, the Springboks might as well have been playing with 14 men. Le Roux had no real interest in rugby, just in doing physical damage. Most tests you play are fairly physical and rough, but in Dunedin it was actually quite dirty, with a lot of kicking.

When it came to the second test we really thought, "We don't want to lose to these guys, because they're not as good a footballers as we are, and the game's moved on from the way they play it." We basically knew they weren't as skilled individually as we were, and they didn't have the weapons in their armoury to knock us over.

The only way they could possibly do it was if we tried to meet fire with fire, and lost our focus. If that situation arose, who knows what the reaction of a referee might be?

So it was just a matter of playing our own game, winning good ball, attacking them, and keeping some pressure on them. We knew that even if things didn't go our way initially, as long as they weren't getting into the game they'd get frustrated and give away penalties.

I didn't even know about the ear biting until after the game. When Fitzy went down I just got the guys into a huddle, and started talking about what we'd do next. In a test match, you don't really take too much notice of those sort of incidents. It's not a situation where Fitzy comes back and says, "Hey, this guy's bitten my ear."

After the test Pinetree had arranged with their manager, Jannie Englebrecht, for all the players, just the players, to get together in the South Africans' hotel. We had the chance to have a yarn about things together away from a large crowd, and most of the officials. It was a great idea, and there was certainly no ill feeling about the Le Roux affair.

We had talked about it briefly in the changing room, but it wasn't the huge issue it became. I guess what grabbed the attention was that it was such a malicious, and bizarre, thing to do.

At the third test in Auckland we had the chance to do something no All Black team has ever done before, to clean sweep a series against the Springboks.

We got to 18-all, but we couldn't finish them off. Over time there's almost a feeling of deja vu about those situations. You know you can win a game, but you're not ahead on the scoreboard. In my experience you revert to the basics of the game. You think of the fundamentals that will put you in a position to deliver the winning blow.

It's like tennis, when you're receiving, and have the chance to break in a vital game. You concentrate on your footwork, and hitting the ball when it bounces at the highest point from the serve, so you can make an attacking shot to put the server under pressure. From there you've put yourself in a position to actually deliver a winning blow. If you attack the net you can volley a winner.

The process is methodical. You're creating the situation to score a try in rugby, to knock a guy out in boxing, or to put a volley into the corner of a tennis court. You take some fairly broad skills and refine them for the winning edge.

In rugby union it's much the same, I think. But there was a difference between the great All Black teams of the 1980s, and the All Black model of 1994. At Eden Park, with the game tied up, we had the Springboks under pressure. In the past we'd have got up there, worked a blindside move, and scored. I could see by the look in Fitzy's eyes that he was thinking the same thing.

But whether it was a lack of killer instinct in us as a team, or the skill level, or other players not having that sense of what we were trying to do, we ended up giving away a penalty, they cleared it, and the chance was gone.

The test did bring Michael Jones back into the test arena for the first time in '94. Blair Larsen was injured, and when Michael came off the reserves bench I went to blindside flanker, and Michael to openside.

Until then I'd been on the openside, and there had been a certain amount of flak flying about that. Laurie told me at the start of the season that with both French tests being on Sundays he wanted me to play openside flanker in the trials.

His reasoning was that with Michael Jones unavailable because of his beliefs, we needed three tall loose forwards who can all jump at the back of the lineout. That's the way international loose forwards are going these days, and the French were certainly no exception. So I had the chance to train for the position, and I was quite happy with my form there in the trials.

Critics suggested I didn't have the speed to play openside flanker, but I really believe speed is not as important to performing well in the position as reading the game as it evolves, and most important of all, your forward pack having dominance.

When you're an openside flanker in a dominant pack it's the best position in the world to play. You end up, with the No 8, being a link between the forwards and the backs, and doing a lot of running with the ball.

But in the French series we really struggled in the first test, and any loose forward will tell you that when your tight five is battling you end up getting sucked into the tight five.

Ask Duane Monkley, the Waikato openside flanker. In 1992 and 1993 we constantly heard that he should be in the All Blacks. But in 1994 we never heard that suggestion. He wasn't playing any better or worse, it was just that in '94 he had to go in and help his tight forwards compete. In the past they were so good they could hold six, or seven, or eight, of the opposing pack, and he was able to roam free.

When there is criticism, I'll look at it. If I think it's something I could use to better my game I'll have a talk with my coaches, my fellow loosies and fellow forwards. If the criticism is warranted, I'd be silly not to take it on board.

No matter how strong the criticism is, it won't irritate me much. I'm a bit like Laurie. If it's a person who I don't respect as having a knowledge of the game it won't bother me at all. It bothers Bev more than anyone because it feels like a personal attack on me. If it comes from an individual I respect for their knowledge of rugby, I will take it on board, and probably even get a little bit upset if I don't agree with it.

*   *   *

Laurie Mains: The criticism of Mike at openside flanker in '94 was from people who didn't stop and study the game. I thought he played extremely well.

To say he wasn't getting out wide and snaffling the ball on the ground was a bloody nonsense. Usually our backs weren't able to get the ball wide. When they did, he was there.

People suggested that Laurent Cabannes was beating him to the loose ball. Whenever that happened it was because Mike was making a tackle. His tackle count in the French tests was astounding. If he's just made a tackle, and it isn't Cabannes, then of course Cabannes will beat him to that loose ball.

But if you look at the ruck and maul statistics, we cleaned out France and South Africa in a big way. If the openside flanker wasn't doing his job, that wouldn't have been the case.

I reject criticism of Mike's play at openside flanker. Through the four complete tests he played in the position (in 1994) he would have been our most consistent player. Having said that, I'm not suggesting he's better there than Michael Jones. I am satisfied he's better than the next options we had.

Mike showed it in the trials in '94. Go back to the Gisborne trial when he was opposing Zinny. They were really 50/50 in that game. Maybe Zinny had a sight edge. Maybe.

Then, when Zinny went off, and Mark Carter came on, Mike cleaned him out. Wide, close, lineout, you name it, Mike cleaned him out. In everything. How quickly people forget.

We do see the best out of Mike when he's playing with people of a similar rugby intelligence to him. When you saw Zinny and him and Michael Jones together in the second half of the third test against South Africa, and then in the Australian test, you could see what I'm talking about.

It wasn't as if they'd played a lot together as a trio. But it was the intelligence level on the field that made them work so well together, and understand each other.

Mike is a marvellous player for continuity. A prime example was the great try scored by Frank Bunce in the test in Sydney on 1992. Like Michael and Zinny, Mike can see things developing in the embryo stage, and be there at a crucial time.

When I first had Mike for Otago he was a No. 8. The reason I changed him was that when Alex Wyllie first became an All Black selector we were talking in Tom Doocey's pub in Christchurch before a Canterbury-Otago game.

Alex said as far as he was concerned Mike wasn't an aggressive or strong enough runner to be at No. 8. You have to keep in mind that Alex had Dale Atkins at No. 8 for his Canterbury teams, and Buck Shelford there for the All Blacks.

I said to Alex, "Where would you see Mike?" And Alex said, "Blindside." So I started playing Mike there, for his sake, in Otago, and that opened the door for Brent Pope to establish himself as the No. 8 in Otago.

Overall, I think blindside is Mike's best position. He perhaps doesn't have the explosive quickness over 20 metres anymore to be an openside flanker. But I accept that he played a lot of rugby in the All Blacks for Alex at openside when Michael Jones was injured, and he played awfully well there.

I also think we're moving away a bit internationally from the power game at No 8, the Buck Shelford/Arran Pene style. Mike could go back and be a hell of a good international No. 8 again. With his style of continuity and his ball skills, his interchange with the halfback would be very strong. I really think he could be a very good No. 8 again.

*   *   *

The one-off Bledisloe Cup test against the Wallabies in Sydney was a first in many respects. It was a mid-week game, and it was under lights. It was hard to understand what the reasoning was for that.

*   *   *

Laurie Mains: The night test was a shaft of the All Blacks. Originally that test was scheduled for a Saturday, and there was a question whether it would be played at night or not.

I argued against it being a night game. It was going to be only two weeks after the third Springbok test, and we had no time to prepare for what was a different circumstance. There were medical papers to support the view that there were physiological changes between playing at 2.30 in the afternoon, and playing at 9.30 at night, which is what it was when you allowed for the time difference from New Zealand. We would have had no opportunity to train properly for the time difference.

Then a report came out of Australia saying that to avoid clashing with coverage of the Commonwealth Games in Australia, they wanted to bring the game forward to the Wednesday night, just 10 days after our last Springbok test.

The New Zealand council instructed the chairman to go to Sydney and argue for the Saturday afternoon game. I was given a categorical assurance by Eddie Tonks, and George Verry (the NZRFU's chief executive officer) that the ONLY fallback position was that it would go to a Saturday night, and on the previous Sunday night we would play a warm-up game under lights against a team such as Australian Universities, a comfortable game to get the guys used to lights and to keep them fit. There was no way they would agree to a Wednesday test.

When we were on the tour to Britain (at the end of 1993) we found out that we were playing on the Wednesday night.

*   *   *

They didn't want us on the field until five minutes before the kick-off in Sydney, but we came out early to have about 15 minutes getting adjusted to the lights. The first half was played at a pretty high tempo, with the ball in play quite a lot, and it always feels like the clock is going quickly when you're playing catch-up. Jason Little took a bomb and scored after 17 seconds, and at halftime we were down 17-6.

Even at that stage, the game was always there for the taking. After the hard matches we'd been through in New Zealand against France and South Africa we were a lot fitter than the Australians, so in the second half we were able to pressure them by throwing caution to the wind, to a degree.

It wasn't really rugby the way you'd want to train and prepare for it, because a lot of the time we weren't making yards from second phase. We were going across field before we were starting to break the line.

What it came down to was the guys saying, "We've got nothing to lose, let's show our natural flair." We really wanted to attack them with the ball in hand, the way we did with Walter (Little), Jeff (Wilson), Shane (Howarth) and Buncy. There was a wee bit of direction in getting position on the field, and not panicking too much.

In some ways the whole of the second half was based on ball maintenance and continuity, which is really what the All Blacks in the 1987-90 era did, supporting the ball carrier. Where we didn't match the teams of the golden era was in the fact the forwards in Sydney didn't always provide the support player to carry on the ball.

So we put the Aussies under pressure, but they were holding and holding, and, even when cracks started to appear, they were able to hold on long enough to take the game.

It was the end of an unusual year for the All Blacks. I began to sense that for some of the All Blacks rugby was just a means to an end. It had almost become a stepping stone from which to launch themselves into a career with a professional sport, rugby league.

To be competitive on the international rugby scene the guys have to train as if it's a professional sport. But they're not getting the professional rewards.

For all the speculation about how much money the All Blacks make, a player who signed a good rugby league contract was making five times what an All Black would, even in the days before the Superleague, so it had to be an attractive proposition.

What that can lead to is players not out there playing for the others in the team, but playing for themselves. Polishing up the CV for the job application, in other words.

Then, if they can look good, even in a losing All Black side, it's not too bad for them. They're quite happy about it. That has to be a concern in the future if rugby union doesn't move, and the money in the Superleague gets even bigger.

In '93 and '94 I even began to sense that about John Timu. Now JT's a good mate and a very good footballer. But when it came to losing tests, I could see it in his face, it wasn't hurting him the way it should.

While one eye is on possible league contracts, some of today's players also suffer from a "me first, the team second" mentality. From a very early stage some players have a hand out, waiting for it to be filled.

I worry too about the ability of some of our younger players to take a setback. Whether it's a knock from the coach at training in front of the side, or a setback when they don't make a test side, they start to create a perception in their own minds that the coach doesn't like them. That it's a personal thing, not a mater of footballing ability.

They don't look at it and say, "I'm better than the player who's got my place, and I'm going to keep coming back until they have to pick me."

At the All Black camp in Auckland in December, '94, I said, "I'm pointing at a lot of you young guys. You've got what's commonly talked about in boxing as glass jaw. One punch and you're down on the canvas, and you don't get up." They're not mentally hardened enough to take a few knockbacks and come back.

I said, "Zinny and I came through an All Black era where we had to train our butts off, and play out of our skins every time we played to even have a chance of getting in ahead of Buck Shelford, AJ Whetton and Michael Jones. And really, no matter how hard we played, and, at times, I thought I was playing better than one or two, if not all of them, you didn't get picked.

"But if you adopted an attitude that the coach didn't like you, you might as well have given it away." I fear there's a mentality growing that if you don't get there straight away you feel there's a vendetta against you, which leads to a bit of in-house fighting, and before long is picked up by the media.

A classic example of how things can go wrong, or be approached the right way, is with midweek teams. The only way a midweek team stays a midweek team, and becomes a problem, is if the players create the situation themselves.

If you mentally place yourself there, and start talking about it, it becomes ingrained. You start drawing a line between two elements in the team. Whenever I've gone on tour, even with Shelford and Whetton and Jones, I made it my goal to play all the tests on tour. That's what I was striving for. But as soon as you regard yourself as a midweeker, that's where you'll stay.

It happened in '93 in Britain. The guys who weren't playing the tests saw themselves as poor second cousins. A lot of the talk when I came into the side over the top of the midweek team came from the fact the midweek side was already set in place.

As far as I'm concerned, if I was coaching or managing a side, I wouldn't pick any player who didn't consider himself good enough to be in a test side.

They wouldn't be worth taking away on tour, because they wouldn't train hard enough physically, which wouldn't make them hard enough mentally. Then, if they do get a bit of a bollocking, or a bit of a knockback, they look to pull the pin and go to league. Some end up blaming the rugby fraternity, or the coach, for what's really their own fault.

It doesn't have to be like that. Joe Stanley's attitude when he played for Auckland, fighting to get into the All Blacks, or Buck Shelford's approach while Murray Mexted held the position Buck coveted at No. 8 in the All Blacks, show what real grit and character is about.

6

Fate Plays a Hand

My wife, Bev, is a great believer in fate. And certainly, when you look at the story that led to us meeting each other, falling in love, marrying, and now being the parents of a growing baby boy, Harrison Patrick, destiny must have played a role.

We travelled on a plane together, without actually speaking, on Sunday, November 5, 1989.

I was with the All Blacks, dragging ourselves onto a Ryanair flight from Cardiff to Dublin, the morning after we'd beaten Wales at Cardiff Arms Park. We were tired, bleary, hungover, and sleepy, but I did notice that one of the flight attendants was a very attractive Irishwoman. By rights, she shouldn't have been on the flight.

*　　*　　*

Bev Brewer: I was about to go out for a Saturday girls' night out in Dublin. I got a call from rostering to say I had to work an early morning flight the next day, to fill in for someone who couldn't make it. It was most unusual. I'd been promoted to supervisor, and seniors very rarely got called back.

I tried to argue my way out of it. "I'm going out with my girlfriends, couldn't you get anyone else?"

But they insisted. They'd been told to get me. I rang around other attendants, but no luck.

I rang back, and asked who we were taking. They said a rugby team. That made me feel even worse. No offence to rugby players, but my brother Jason and his friends played the game, and I knew that in a group they got pretty lively.

When I was told it was the All Blacks that meant little to me either. I thought it must be a team from Africa visiting Wales and Ireland.

So my night out with the girls was very quiet, and before the sun was coming up I was on my way out to the airport.

Jason was just coming home from a Saturday night out.

"What are you away so early for Bev, I thought you had the weekend off?"

I told him I'd been called in for a flight with the All Blacks. Jason was thrilled. They were an amazing team. He wished he was going on the flight to talk rugby with them.

When we got to Cardiff we were about 90 minutes late leaving. There was the usual mountain of gear that goes with a rugby team, plus a large amount of television equipment.

Finally the players started coming on board. The first one I saw was Buck Shelford. My God! He was an enormous man. The rest shuffled on, and most dozed off when they hit their seats. It had obviously been a big night out in Cardiff.

There was nothing untoward about any of the behaviour, but a couple of the Samoan boys in the team called each other with the kissing sound they make to attract attention from a friend. Not understanding then that it was a perfectly innocent gesture, and nothing to do with us, the attendants, we were highly offended. We spent most of the trip behind a curtain at the back of the plane talking about them. They would have been pretty lucky to get even an orange drink during the flight. We got to Dublin, and they were off to the Burlington Hotel. Bye Bye, All Blacks.

*   *   *

We got into the lift at the hotel, and there was a poster behind glass of a woman modelling traditional Irish clothes. She looked very familiar. I looked closer. It was our flight attendant, the attractive blonde Irishwoman. For the next two days I noticed her everytime we went in the lift.

*   *   *

Bev Brewer: Ronnie Cosgrave, a very successful club owner in Dublin, was having a fancy dress party, and he invited several of us to come to his club. It was something of a media event, and quite late in the evening I was settled talking with my girlfriends, when Ronnie came and asked if I'd come to the foyer for one more photograph.

I went out, and there were several of the All Blacks, the dirty dirties, as I now know they're called, not needed as players or reserves, for the next game. Mike was one of them. We struck a chord right away, and a couple of weeks later, when I went to London for a holiday with my mother, Mike asked if I'd come to Italy with him. I didn't go then, but he came to Dublin to have Christmas with us.

I suppose you'd call it a long distance romance during 1990, conducted by telephone and letters. It wasn't easy, and during the year we virtually stopped writing to each other.

*   *   *

The All Blacks toured France at the end of 1990, and I tried to ring Bev from Paris, to see her in Dublin before I went back to New Zealand. I got Jason, and he said that Bev was on holiday in America. I decided to go to Dublin anyway, with a few other All Blacks.

*   *   *

Bev Brewer: Here's where fate plays a part. I wasn't really enjoying the American trip, so I cut it short and came home. I had no idea Mike was in Dublin, but I was still missing him.

Mike and the boys were at Ronnie's, and a girlfriend of mine told Mike that I was back from America. We finally caught up with each other, and we knew then that we loved each other.

Mike asked me to come to New Zealand for a holiday. He told me that if I saw the country, I'd love it. I arrived for Valentine's Day, 1991, and we went to some of the most beautiful places in New Zealand. We wandered through Queenstown, stayed in a little cottage at Whangamata, at the base of the Coromandel, and enjoyed the beach, and the summer. I did love the country.

*   *   *

I wanted Bev to return to live in New Zealand, and she agreed. First she had to go back to Ireland and break the news.

*   *   *

Bev Brewer: It was a traumatic time. I broke the news to my parents, and my friends, and two months later, after shedding many, many tears, flew back to Dunedin.

Dublin was where I was born, and had grown up. Both my parents, Peter and Anne, were involved in entertainment. My mother is a professional singer and actress who also teaches singing in the London Studio Centre, while my father is a singer and compere and comedian in a cabaret in a large Dublin hotel.

When I was growing up my mother insisted I have piano and singing lessons, but it wasn't really what I enjoyed, and by the time I left Sancta Maria College in Dublin, when I was 18, I'd decided the piano wasn't for me. For eight years I worked for fashion houses as both a catwalk and photographic model, fitting the modelling work around my job with Ryanair from 1988.

My brother, Jason, is four years younger than me, and, once the normal squabbles over sweets during infancy were over, we became very close. He's one of my dearest friends now, and being apart from each other has made us even more aware of the affection there is between us.

Luckily, I've been able to get back to see my family and friends on a fairly regular basis. It was one of the promises Mike made when we decided to get married, that whenever it was possible, I'd get back to Ireland to visit.

It is a different lifestyle in Ireland, especially in Dublin. So much revolves around getting together with friends, having a few drinks, going out for dinner, and staying out much later than is the norm in New Zealand.

Usually I cope with homesickness, but the one thing that breaks my heart is Christmas. It is just so alien to what I'm used to. In Ireland we have cold, dark weather in December, and it's a time for wrapping up in front of the fire. It's such a huge change to see people surfing on Christmas Day, or having a barbie for their Christmas dinner.

*   *   *

I was born in Pukekohe on November 6, 1964. Mum and Dad were living in Paerata then, and Dad was driving for the Paerata Dairy Company. I have one older brother, Kevin, who was born in 1962.

Before I went to school we shifted to Pukekohe, and my parents, Dick and Joan, have lived there ever since. Dick played for Counties when they started as a province, back in 1955, when they were called South Auckland Counties. He played No 8 and lock, and I've had people he played his football with describe him as usually being the hard man of the team. My mother was a good sportsperson too, playing netball in the winter and tennis in summer.

I'm of Maori descent on both sides of my family, a fact that many people don't realise. The Southern Maori selectors certainly do though, and for about five years in a row I was asked to be available for the Southern Maori team. I never did, which was purely a case of priorities. From the time I left high school I've either been going to university or working.

My priorities in rugby went club, province, the All Blacks, and between them there was barely time for study or work. I would have liked to play Maori rugby as well, but as niggling injuries started to come along I really think I would have finished up tipping over in four or five years if I'd added Maori rugby to the list. I just couldn't do everything.

Much of my early life in Pukekohe revolved around playing as much sport as I could, and getting by doing just enough homework to keep out of serious trouble. At primary and intermediate school I was probably keener on athletics than I was on rugby. When I was at intermediate school I represented Auckland at a Trans Tasman meeting in Sydney as a high jumper, and actually won the event. I wasn't that tall for my age, but I was pretty lean, and before I left school I'd jumped 1.98m (about 6ft 6in).

The greatest gift my parents gave me was their support with my sport. Athletics is very time consuming, and on many weekends I'd be competing on both Saturday and Sunday. Mum and Dad would always take me to the meetings, whether they were on the North Shore, or in Manurewa. Kevin was more into his tennis, which was nearer to home, and looking back I can see that he was often left on his own while we travelled the greater Auckland area.

It was when I was at Pukekohe High School, as I started getting bigger, that rugby started to take over from athletics, and swimming, and tennis, and any other sport. I'd always played the game, in the backs until the fourth form, but when I made the first XV in my fifth form year it became a bit more than something I really enjoyed because you trained and played the game with your mates. In my last year I captained the first XV.

My parents' support came through again with rugby. I made Counties school and age group teams, then regional teams, and finally a New Zealand Secondary School team. Dad would offer advice if I asked for it, but neither he nor Mum ever ranted and raved about sport the way I saw some parents do.

Dad would only go so far as to say that I should keep my running up for rugby. "If you're fit, you can do anything." The rest of the time they were just very supportive.

The New Zealand secondary school team of '81 was an interesting one. It was selected, but didn't go to Japan when sponsorship fell through. In the aftermath of the Springbok tour that year some firms didn't want to be associated with rugby.

Mark Finlay, the Manawatu and All Black fullback, Paul Henderson, and Sean Fitzpatrick were all in the squad, and one lock was a fiery forward from Auckland Grammar, who would later concentrate on cricket, test batsman Mark Greatbatch.

In my first year out of school, 1982, I headed to Australia for a year's working holiday. My first stop was Melbourne for a friend's wedding, where I applied for a job with an insurance company. The wage on offer was $106 a week.

That didn't appeal, so I booked a bus ticket from Melbourne to Port Hedland, in Western Australia. For three days I travelled non-stop, through Adelaide, across the Nullabor to Perth, and then 24 hours north to Port Hedland.

My aim was to save enough money to pay my way through

university. I didn't want to have to rely on Mum and Dad, or be in a situation where they might feel I'd wasted their money if I dropped out.

The best money in Port Hedland was at the Mt Newman Mining Company, but you had to be 18 to work there. I had a stroke of luck. The only football being played was with the Hedland Hawks league team, and I'd joined up with them. I told the company personnel officers I'd lost my passport to prove I was 18, and the Hawks' coach, Kerry Day, backed me up.

I worked in the locomotive workshops at the port. They used to rail iron ore in from the mine to be shipped out. At the workshops we'd hoist the engine out of the locomotives, strip it, dip it in an acid bath, and get all the muck and grease off it. Then we'd help the fitters recondition the motors. It wasn't that different from working for New Zealand Rail, and not as dirty as it sounds.

It was also very lucrative. You could earn as much as $800 a week with overtime, and the single men's quarters were like the Sheraton, if the Sheraton only charged $68 a fortnight. The food was superb, your room was serviced every day, and in 10 months I was able to save about $NZ12,000.

I enjoyed playing league. For the Hawks I was a fullback or centre, and it was probably where I learned most of my tackling skills. League is a very different game to rugby, much more stop-start, and we did a lot of hard work on the beach at Port Hedland, going up and back, up and back for anaerobic training.

It was a lot of fun, but there were some hard nuts in the north west. We played a team that was mainly big Christmas Islanders, who worked out on the north-west shelf. I went to step inside a forward, and he stuck his elbow out, catching me right up under my nose. I woke up three hours later in hospital, and didn't play for six weeks.

I just got back in time for the semifinals, and then we were up against the same team in the final. The forward who elbowed me was still there. A good mate of mine was a big Tongan called Bunny, who was a pretty good boxer.

About the second minute of the game Bunny said to me, "I'm

going to get this guy." The forward took the ball up, and Bunny hit him with a tackle across the chest that made your eyes cross just looking at it.

It was quite legal, but just so hard that he knocked the guy out. Bunny strolled back and gave me a quiet wink. We'd lost to them in the first and second rounds, but we won the final. That was a big thing in the north-west, and we partied at the Hedland Hotel for two full days.

Kerry Day, the coach, had played for St George in Sydney league, and a scout offered me a trial for St George at the end of the season. It shows how much things have changed, that in '82 I didn't really know what the Winfield Cup was. In any case, I was much more interested in getting home, going to University, and trying to play provincial rugby.

The next out of the ordinary offer I would get to play football also came in Australia, during the 1988 All Black tour.

Several of us in that team had both Maori and Dalmatian ancestry. There was Kevin Boroevich, Frano Botica, and, when I was in the card school, Mike Brewerovitch. In fact, everything carried a "vitch" for us. You went to get a drinkovitch. You ate an ice creamovitch.

One afternoon we were playing cards in the groupovitch, and a guy phoned for me, and said he was ringing to see if Frano Botica and I would be interested in playing rugby in Italy.

The man's name was Boris Porkovitch.

I went, "Yeah, good one Boris." And hung up.

He rang again. It had to be one of the guys. Down went the phone again.

Finally another player came to the door. Boris was on the phone, and he appeared to be a real person.

Eventually Frano and I did meet Boris, and it was a stroke of good fortune for us. Boris was an Australian, but he spoke fluent Italian, and he was coaching a team in L'Aquila, a town of about 80,000 people to the north-east of Rome, just half an hour from the Italian Alps.

We had a good relationship with Boris. His philosophy was that he wanted to learn as much as he could off us, so we gave him ideas as far as coaching drills were concerned.

Then, when it came to talk to the team, because we were still learning Italian, it looked as if the ideas had come from the coach, which was the way Frano and I wanted it, and was a lot more successful.

The one training habit we couldn't stand was the opposed training on a Thursday. We had our air fares paid, and accommodation and meals provided. It was a comfortable life. The locals were actually paid per game, and some for going to training. But the game payment was only made if they actually made the playing 15, and there were about 60 people in the squad.

So at times the "training" on Thursday night was more demanding than the game on Sunday, as players fought to get into the team. Guys were being injured all the time in opposed training. The Italians did it because it was what the French did. We hated it, and eventually were able to flag it altogether.

In the two years that we were there we lost just one game at home. But it was a very different story when we travelled. At home you played with 15 men, but when you travelled it was sometimes the two foreigners against the rest.

I think that what people, family and friends, think of them is extremely important to the Italians. They'll give it everything when playing in front of people that matter to them, but flag it away when they're not. We beat one team in L'Aquila 75-4, but when we played them away from home we actually lost 15-10. It was incredible.

The whole process of travelling away was bizarre to Kiwi eyes. Most of the rugby in Italy is played in the north, so, being in central Italy, we'd often be eight hours on a bus driving up the autostrada to a game.

Frano and I would get a few beers organised for the bus trip home, which rarely saw us back in L'Aquila before 2am, but at first Boris, an Australian remember, was the only one who shared them with us. The Italian guys would sit and read a book, or watch the video on the bus. When we stopped at an autogrill we'd get a cup of coffee, or something to eat. The Italians would get straight to a phone and ring their wife, girlfriend or mother.

We gradually introduced our ways to the team. At first it would just be a cheeky halfback that joined the party, but gradually more and more would have a drink with us, and then they started stocking up with a bit of wine, salami and cheese.

At the start of the season Frano and I would roll off the bus a bit. The Italians would walk off cold sober. But by the time we were on the last trip before Christmas, Frano and I came out of the bus as sober as judges. The Italians came lurching out singing and laughing. The music stopped pretty quickly when their partners and mothers saw the condition they were in.

In the first season we had a great year by the usual playing standards of the team. We actually made the semifinals, where we were beaten by Benetton, the team John Kirwan and Craig Green had both played for. When we played them in Treviso we were actually ahead 9-0 after Frano had scored a brilliant try, but then the rain came down, and they beat us 16-9.

Earlier in the year we beat them in L'Aquila. Greeno did a cutback early in the game, and I was able to line him up and really hammer him. From then on it was like our players had grown an extra leg. We knocked them out of the game. At the end the administrators were hugging us, crying with joy.

Frano was a real hero in L'Aquila. He scored brilliant tries, and he was kicking goals as well. It took Frano no time to work out that if we won at home a stroll through town on the Monday morning was a very good idea.

You see, L'Aquila is one of a handful of towns in Italy that's a real rugby stronghold. So after a Sunday game when he'd scored most of the points, if Botsy wandered down the main street in shorts and jandals, and he did, shopkeepers would literally call "Bravo Botica, Bravo Botica" and by the time he went back home he might be fully clothed with a new jacket, trousers and shoes, and be carrying fresh fruit, cheeses, and some bottles of wine. Emotion quickly translated into generosity.

Actually we loved the lifestyle, and not just on Monday mornings. After breakfast Frano and I would go to the gym and train. Then we'd go to the markets in the town square, buy fresh chicken, vegetables, bread and cheese for lunch, have a leisurely lunch, and then the traditional Italian siesta. At 3.30 in the afternoon we'd go to team training, which could go on until 5.30 or 6pm. We might meet some of the administrators, or other players, and go out for a dinner at about 8 o'clock, which would rarely finish before midnight.

Everything for the Italians was based around family and friends, making time for people. When you look at New Zealand now you realise that everybody is so busy we don't make the time for friends to the extent that we should.

There was another benefit in L'Aquila too. From the room of the apartment I could look out and see the mountains. If the weather was good, and the snow cover was deep, we could be skiing by 8am.

The next season wasn't so much fun. Brad Johnstone, the former All Black prop, joined as coach, and in his first season he struggled to get to grips with the culture of rugby in Italy.

He was into old school training. Run them off their feet, and if they don't like it, run them harder. That can work with a New Zealand team, where it's considered a sign of weakness to say the training is too tough.

In L'Aquila it led to a players' strike. In that second season we made the quarter-finals, and Brad took us to an Adriatic Coast resort for a four day training camp. The regime was tough. Up in the morning, train at 7 o'clock, then breakfast. Train before lunch, and then train again in the afternoon. It was raining a lot, and we spent a lot of time running on wet sand.

After three days the players came to Frano and me.

"Our legs are dead," they said. "We're going on strike."

They called a meeting with the administrators, and we went home early. We played in L'Aquila, and for the only time in the two years Frano and I were there, we lost at home.

That wasn't the perfect end to two fascinating years, but, while I enjoyed Italy so much I could happily live there for several years, in the next New Zealand summer there was something more important to do, to show Bev why we could enjoy making a life together in New Zealand.

*   *   *

Bev Brewer: When I came back to Dunedin the way was made easier for me by some girlfriends who I clicked with straight away. Susan Malthus, who had been flatting with Mike, soon became, and remains, a close friend, as does Nicki O'Donnell, who, with Susan, would be a bridesmaid at our wedding.

The whole rugby scene was new to me. To be honest, in Dublin, when I was a schoolgirl, a few of us might go to watch a game, but we were only there to check out the good looking boys.

Because it was such a new experience, I found it very interesting, at times more so than some New Zealand women, who have seen the game be such a big factor in their lives for as long as they can remember.

Before I left Dublin someone said to me that in New Zealand if I was walking down the street with Mike Brewer it'd be like walking through Dublin with Jackie Charlton, the Irish soccer coach. I didn't really believe them until we went into a hotel in Wellington for a drink and a meal. In the bar people swarmed up for autographs, and then when we were eating, people came up just wanting to shake hands. By comparison I doubt that an Irish rugby international would be recognised by 90 per cent of the general public in Ireland.

In August, 1991, Mike went to Sydney for a speech. When he returned he had an engagement ring. There wasn't a formal proposal as such, but once I had come to Dunedin to live Mike started using phrases like "when we're married" and "it'd be nice to go there when we're married."

We moved to Christchurch in the winter of '92, so the last months before we were married in Dunedin, on January 9, 1993, were hectic. Susan and Nicki held the fort in Dunedin, and I started travelling down almost every weekend to help with the preparations.

Our wedding day itself was a wonderful time. My parents, and my brother Jason, were there, and my mother sang beautifully during the service at St Joseph's Cathedral, conducted by Father Michael Tobin, from Dublin.

Joe Stanley was Mike's best man, and his brother, Kevin, the groomsman. Susan and Nicki were my bridesmaids, and little Hannah Cooper, Greg and Sam's daughter, was the flowergirl.

It was a wonderful day. We had friends from Mike's university days, rugby friends, players and coaches and administrators, friends from Dunedin, our families, and a special treat for me, a dear friend from Dublin, Emma Ellis, who had travelled to New Zealand just for the wedding.

On our way to Larnach's Castle, where we continued our celebrations, we suddenly pulled into a Liquor King wholesalers. Joe rushed inside, and returned with glasses and a bottle of champagne. He said he'd felt a little nervous, and needed something to calm him down.

Most of the people at Larnach's Castle had been in Dunedin for several days, and by the time the party was properly underway virtually everyone knew everybody else. The band played through the night, and Mike and I finally left by 4am. I believe people were still being persuaded to leave at 5am.

*   *   *

It was the best wedding I've ever been to. As time went by there was everything from Arran Pene modelling a woman's hat to AJ Whetton trying to play the bass guitar.

At one stage Grizz Wyllie wanted Phil Gifford to have another rum with him, and was emphasising the point by hitting him on the head with an empty glass. Phil kept refusing, so Grizz turned his attention to Simon Barnett.

"You'll have a bloody drink, won't you?"

Simon did. Then another one. He could see this game might never end, and he was getting desperate.

"Alex," he croaked, "would you like to dance with my wife?"

Luckily for Simon, and his wife, Jodi, Grizz turned out to be a bit of a twinkletoes on the floor.

*   *   *

Bev Brewer: The most exciting thing that has ever happened for Mike or myself was the arrival of Harrison Patrick Brewer, a healthy, handsome baby boy on March 22, 1995.

He is totally the light of our lives, and puts any disappointments that have come to us in the past in perspective.

In his rugby career Mike has suffered some cruel blows, but says now that they fade to nothing when he holds Harrison. We didn't really know it until Harrison was born, but he is what makes our lives complete.

Not one of my fondest memories - on the sideline at the All Black trials in Napier in 1992 nursing a torn calf muscle. Michael Beauchamp, Photosport

A good finish to a great tour in 1989. We beat the Barbarians 21-10, but it was really the end of a golden era.

Photosport

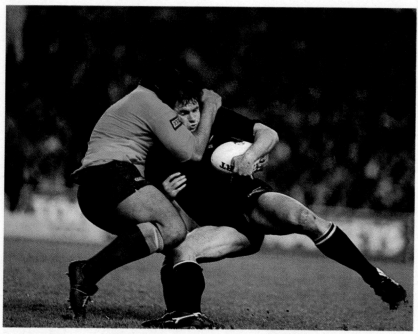

Technically it's not the perfect tackle by Willie Ofahengaue but it did the job, something we couldn't quite manage under lights against Australia in Sydney in 1994.

David Rogers, Allsport

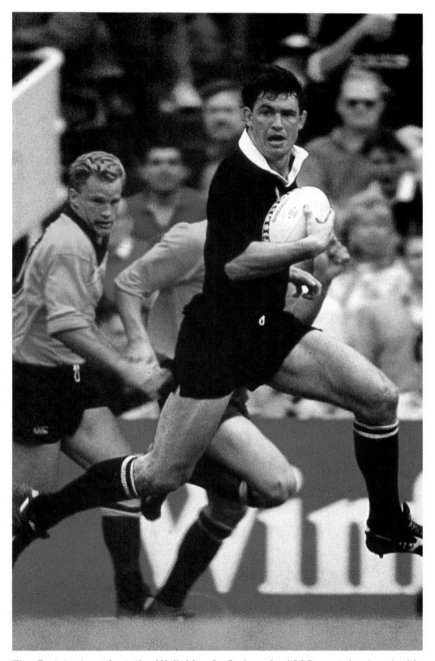

The first test against the Wallabies in Sydney in 1992 contained a double dose of frustration for me. We lost by one point and I injured my shoulder which kept me out of the rest of the tour, including the ground breaking trip to South Africa.

Andrew Cornaga, Photosport

Back on old schoolboy territory with Otago, playing Counties in 1992 at Pukekohe Stadium.

Andrew Cornaga, Photosport

The game of continuity we developed in Otago, this time against North Harbour in 1992.

Andrew Cornaga, Photosport

In 1992 Graeme Bachop, Richard Loe and I went to the All Black trials in Napier full of optimism. Richard's was well justified. Selection decisions and injury would make it a less memorable All Black season for Graeme and me.

Andrew Cornaga, Photosport

Buck Shelford considers his lineout options for North Harbour against Otago in 1990. In 1988 some of the Otago players went over the top in their determination to stop Buck.

Andrew Cornaga, Photosport

Otago made a couple of spirited challenges for the Ranfurly Shield at Eden Park without managing to ever prise it away from the mighty Aucklanders. This scene from the 1992 game which Auckland won 16-11.

Andrew Cornaga, Photosport

It wasn't a happy time for Otago at Rugby Park in Hamilton in the 1992 national provincial championship final. The Waikato players came out with a glassy-eyed look I'd last seen in Nantes in 1986.

Troy Restieaux, Photosport

It might not be as quick as Graeme Bachop's pass, but the ball is on the move in the Gisborne trial of 1994. Andrew Cornaga, Photosport

Trying to get things moving against France in 1994 at Lancaster Park, but on that day we just never got a roll on.
Andrew Cornaga, Photosport

Counting down against France in 1994 at Eden Park. We would be beaten by a try two minutes from fulltime.
Andrew Cornaga, Photosport

The 1994 All Black trial in Gisborne was the start of a programme not many of us were looking forward to. Six tests in less than eight weeks is not a dream schedule.

Andrew Cornaga, Photosport

Readying myself for training with my new team Canterbury, after my move north from Dunedin in 1993. Matt Greenslade, Photosport

Facing the media with coach Vance Stewart after Canterbury's game against the Springboks in 1994. We'd lost. Andrew Cornaga, Photosport

Joining Canterbury in 1993 was an eye opener. In many ways the team seemed doomed to fail.

Matt Greenslade, Photosport

Waikato struggled to match Canterbury when we went to Hamilton in 1994 for the Ranfurly Shield challenge. After 15 minutes I knew we were never going to be beaten.

Troy Restieaux, Photosport

It's a good feeling winning the Ranfurly Shield. Sharing my delight after the defeat of Waikato in Hamilton are Grant Kelly and Mark McAtamney.

Andrew Cornaga, Photosport

Plenty of feeling going into the haka, led by Zinzan Brooke, before the third test against the Springboks at Eden Park in 1994. Andrew Cornaga, Photosport

High stepping our way through an All Black training in 1994. From left: Ian Jones, Robin Brooke, Zinzan Brooke, Blair Larsen, Richard Loe, Olo Brown, me and Sean Fitzpatrick. Andrew Cornaga, Photosport

We had the second test against France at Eden Park in 1994 sewn up, but we lacked the killer punch.

Andrew Cornaga, Photosport

On the rampage against Canada at Eden Park in 1995. In a prelude of things to come at the World Cup, we ran up 73 points.

Andrew Cornaga, Photosport

7

No Prima Donnas

One key to an ego free climb is that the team must be more important than the individual. We're not talking some misty eyed, Californian hot tub day dream here.

When I was appointed captain of Otago in 1985 some of the vital men in what would be our ego-free climb probably thought a hot tub was what you boiled your dog tucker in, and a good trip was bringing the ute into the city from Ophir without a puncture.

The Otago forward pack in '85 were all hard men, who played their club rugby in the country and had an ill concealed contempt for "bloody students." I was certainly a scarfie, in my second year of a physical education degree, flatting, playing for University A in the town competition.

During the first year I made the Otago training squad, but never actually got on the field. I made a couple of practices, and then needed an operation on a damaged knee.

In '85 I got a phone call from Laurie Mains, then in his third season as Otago coach.

"Mike, it's Laurie Mains here, I'll be naming you in the Otago squad when it comes out tomorrow. Are you happy about that?"

I certainly was.

"I'd also like to discuss the issue of captaincy with you. I'm planning to make you our captain this season."

Now he had me very apprehensive. The Otago pack was dominated by players like Ken Bloxham, a tough, unyielding hooker, and men of similar attitude and experience, like Andy Hollander and Richard Knight. My first thought was, "What will these country boys think about some 20-year-old hairy arsed student coming in and captaining the team?"

We had a meeting with Laurie and the senior players. The players went through the issue of what pressures would be involved captaining the team, what was required from me, and how they would help me through that first season or two. But I still wasn't happy.

I went back to Laurie after I'd had time to think about the meeting and said I still didn't want the job. By now Laurie and Kenny Bloxham were making it very clear they wanted me to be captain. In the end I decided all I could do was to try, as a much younger person who was captaining the side, to earn the senior players' respect by leading by example.

*   *   *

Laurie Mains: In 1985 Mike had come back fit and strong, and I needed a captain to take over from Wayne Graham. I looked at the senior players, but there wasn't the type of captain and leader I wanted.

As I often did in club rugby, I watched a couple of University A's club games from down on the sideline. I wanted a closer look at the players, and I also wanted to find out what role players took in communication and motivation. Even though Mike wasn't the captain, he was very clearly the motivator, and he quite accurately pinpointed things that needed to be worked on in forward play. I thought, well, very clearly you have to disregard the guy's age in some respects. We've got a pretty mature young man here who already reads a game of rugby well.

I spoke to several of the senior players who were very supportive, and thought it was a good idea. If I felt the player was the right man to be captain, they'd back it to the hilt.

*   *   *

Ken Bloxham: I'd been through the mill as captain myself for a couple of years, on and off, and I didn't want the job again.

98

Laurie wanted me to keep playing, but I told him I didn't want to be captain. As a hooker you don't have the vision of the game you need to be captain. If a back makes a mistake, and you've got your head down in a scrum, how can you say anything to him? I thought it was a great idea to make Mike the captain. He could read things a lot better than someone stuck in the middle of the scrum.

You could already see with Mike that he was a young player with a great deal of ability. It was probably a fairly big ask for a guy that young, but he looked to be one of the most promising loose forwards in the country. I tried to support him as much as I could, and being one of the oldest players I was probably someone people would say things to they were scared to say to Mike or Laurie. I was a bit of a shoulder to cry on, so to speak.

We'd had a couple of tough years, and when I was captaining the side, I felt I was getting the knives put into me. When Mike came along I felt it was only fair I'd be supportive, in the hope that he'd never feel he had the knives and daggers twisting round in his back. It's the people on the perimeter of the team, the heirachy, the media, some of the spectators, who allow the nastiness to creep in. It gets fed back, and you try to ignore it, but it's hard to do that. I thought, well, we're on the way to building something, we've got to get in behind and support him.

*   *   *

So on May 18, 1985, I ran onto Carisbrook, for the first time in the Otago A jersey, against New Zealand Universities. In the programme I was listed as the official captain. But Ken Bloxham was really the on-field captain.

I guess if you wanted to know what a real team man means, in business or in sport, Blocky would be the epitome of it. In his heart what mattered was Otago rugby, and he could see the benefits of me being able to learn from the older players, to get involved in the decision making while I still had the luxury of all the experience around me.

Blocky could see that within one or two years the bulk of the forward pack was going to retire, which could leave me taking over the reins with a lot of inexperienced players, while I was inexperienced myself in decision making as a captain. He had the foresight to see that helping me in the captain's role should be for the good of Otago in the future.

It didn't take long for him to prove how genuine his attitude was. We were on our first trip away in '85, a two match visit to the North Island. Blocky was the sort of guy who would be in bed at 8pm on the first night of the tour. The next night, at 9pm, after a couple of beers. By the end of the trip he'd be bullet proof and unstoppable.

We drew 9-all with Manawatu in Palmerston North, which in those days was a good result for us. I was in my room with John Latta, and at about 1am Blocky and Andy Hollander, with a few on board, decided they wanted to come in.

I called out, "Go to bed, Blocky."

"No," he replied. "Let us in."

"Go away, Blocky."

"Let us in, or we're coming through the door."

The door started to shake and creak as they charged it with their shoulders. John Latta and I were now bracing each side of the door. We were worried they'd take it off the hinges.

Then the banging stopped. Blocky spoke.

"It's your last warning. I'm coming through."

Seconds later there was a mighty, splintering crash. His head appeared, at about hip height, through the shattered panel of the door.

His shoulders weren't inside, just his head. Blocky looked up at us. "I told you I was coming in." Finally he pulled his head back through the hole he'd blasted in the door.

I was shaking, but I dropped my voice as low as it would go and growled, "Blocky, go to bed now, or you'll never play for Otago again."

It would have been a disaster if he'd wanted to be confrontational. But even at that moment, team loyalty came first. He turned round and took off to bed.

*   *   *

Ken Bloxham: Just being a good Otago forward really, putting your head down.

*   *   *

Laurie Mains: I had an idea of the sort of captain I wanted. It wasn't a yes-man to me. He needed to have the confidence to go out and make decisions, and fully understand them. But if he was just coming into first class rugby he'd have no preconceived ideas about captaincy, or about how the game should be played. Without set ideas of his own, he could get to understand the way I thought better, and would therefore be able to be an extension of my discipline and tactical thinking on the paddock.

The guts of our forward pack was made up of good, honest, country lads. With the type of player you might get in first class rugby today it might not work, having such a young captain. But with our forwards then, it was strictly a matter of whether they respected the guy or not. Mike got in and worked even harder than they did. He certainly wasn't a scarfie in the sense of being a prima donna. They were pretty quickly impressed.

*   *   *

Our strength when I started playing for Otago lay with the forwards. We played a very structured type of game, kicking for position on the field through Lindsay Smith or John Haggart at first-five, and Dean Kenny at halfback. Then we tried to force the opposition into mistakes through pressure.

Leading up to a game the tactics were very much driven by Laurie and the senior players. During a game, because the plan was so concise, it didn't take a lot to keep to it. In the early days I probably had a check list of no more than a dozen options, which we weren't supposed to go outside.

Laurie was a real stickler in those early days for keeping to the game plan. Even if you won, but strayed from the agreed plan, you'd get a real bollocking on the Tuesday. Some of the training that Lindsay and John (Haggart) had to endure because they'd changed the plan was quite incredible. After one game against Wairarapa-Bush, when we had a shocker, Lindsay actually ended up in hospital after a training run. The old heart valve had a bit of a flutter.

If things got a bit wayward during a game Blocky would come to me, and he might say, "We've got these guys up front. Let's keep busting up the middle." If we were up against a really tough pack, we'd try to move it round the sides.

I was usually at No 8 in the early years, so the communication ran between Blocky and me, out to Dean Kenny and John Haggart. In the first couple of years we had to eliminate errors as much as possible, because when we played Auckland, Wellington or Canterbury they had bigger packs. If we lost the ball it could take us 10 minutes to win it back again.

*   *   *

Ken Bloxham: In those days the team in general had quite a bit of input, but he had firm control over it on the field. He had the capabilities to do that.

As time went by he became a very good captain. He was fair, but when a decision had to be made he was quite forceful about it. Off the field he had the diplomacy to look after the players. I thought he did a marvellous job actually.

*   *   *

Looking back I would say that Laurie as a coach was very good at summing up his players' abilities, the constraints of their own talent, how they can perform as a side, and then determining the game plan to best suit them to win games.

In 1983, Otago had almost gone down into the second division. Southland missed a kick from in front of the posts that would have seen Otago relegated. So Laurie devised his plan, which kept the ball in front of the forwards, who were good enough to dominate the middle to lower order first division teams, and make sure we stayed in the first division.

*   *   *

Laurie Mains: When I started with the Otago team I used to train them really hard. Mike used to relish it. We had this drill on the scrum and ruck machine that could go on for an hour, and depending on how far apart the machines were it could get tough. Mike used to lead by example with that drill. He was fit, the work was satisfying him, and he believed it was doing the forward pack a lot of good, which it was.

Basically, I think he approved of the training methods in those early days, and that probably led to a fair bit of bonding as captain and coach.

*   *   *

Laurie realised we didn't have a lot of players with the talent that Auckland and Canterbury teams had in the early 80s, so we had to have a side that was very fit, and full of heart. Laurie wasn't gruff at training, the way Grizz Wyllie was, but he was very demanding.

Let me explain about the ruck machine. It was three tackle bags on a sled. We'd begin at a scrum machine, run to the ruck machine, drive into that, then run 30 metres back around the scrum machine, and hit the ruck machine again. So it was like going from a scrum to two rucks in a game, then straight back to the set piece.

I especially remember one cold, wet, stinking night at Kettle Park, which is out by the beach. We must have had a bad game in the weekend, because after a pretty hard run with drills and tackle bags, we moved onto the scrum and ruck machines.

At the beach it's a nightmare, because sand blows onto the bags, and it just rips the skin right off your face. The machines were about 25 metres apart when we began, and the longer we went, the more pissed off Laurie got, and the wilder we got.

We must have gone for 50 minutes doing this, and in the last quarter hour the machines were at opposite sides of the field, so we were having to run the width of the field to get around them. We were whacking into the ruck machine harder and harder, actually trying to break it, though we found out that was impossible.

Finally he called a halt. "Righto, let's get that out of your system, do a couple of laps." The backs were long gone at this stage, they were in the changing shed. Far too cold for backs. We did the laps, and Laurie called, "On the line," and we did about a dozen 120 metre sprints.

We walked back to the shed, and looked at each other. We actually had blood running down the sides of our faces, raw flesh. It certainly hurt, but if you hurt at training and get through it, then if you face the pain barrier in a game you'll kick through. If you train hard enough you won't even get to the pain barrier when you're playing.

At the start I think Laurie still had a few doubts about whether a scarfie could ever match the country forwards for hardness. At the start of the '85 season Laurie would still say to me, "I'd only ever have one scarfie in my forward pack, and that might be one too many."

A year or so later he brought Rob Gordon (who would later play for the All Blacks out of Waikato) into the Otago team, and we started in on the scrum-ruck machine. After about 20 minutes of going at it non-stop, Rob had had enough. He was lying beside the scrum machine, barely showing signs of life. Laurie walked over to him and said, "I **knew** I should only have one scarfie in the pack."

Despite being an All Black fullback in his playing days, Laurie's specific coaching area with Otago was in the forwards. At the start he had Lyn Jaffray, a former All Black five-eighths, helping with the backs. I think Laurie running the forwards stemmed from the fact we had to have the forwards firing in every game, and Laurie wanted to make sure that happened.

He would be one of the best, possibly the best, forward coach I've ever had as far as the technical side goes with rucking, mauling, lineout play, and driving. The highly technical side of scrummaging was the only thing he shied away from, leaving that to the likes of Ken Bloxham, John Latta, Steve Hotton, and, as we got on, Dave Latta. Laurie did get involved in attitude at scrum time, and that is a big part of how a scrum works.

So his role at training would usually be to work with the forwards, and then, when we came together as a team, to run the lot.

*   *   *

Laurie Mains: I didn't have a problem with people helping Mike out on the paddock with tactics. I'd tried Ken Bloxham as a captain, but it just put him off his game. It would have screwed Andy Hollander up too. But as lieutenants they were ideal.

They gave Mike a lot of advice, right through to the end of their careers, and he had the ability and intelligence to channel it.

*   *   *

As a young player one thing I really enjoyed was getting the chance to pit myself against the best provincial players in my position. In 1994, I was in Invercargill when Southland won promotion back to the first division, and some of their supporters were saying, "It's going to be terrible in the first division, we'll get hammered." My attitude was quite different. How can a young player know if he's up to it unless he gets the chance to play against the best?

So in 1985, when we went to Athletic Park to play Wellington, I was really looking forward to marking Murray Mexted, Wellington's No 8 and captain.

Mex was one of those larger than life figures, a brilliant end of the lineout player, the best in the world until AJ Whetton hit his stride. Playing him was certainly the biggest challenge I'd faced to that time.

We went to toss the coin in the dingy, cold tunnel at Athletic Park. Murray came striding out, moustache bristling. Being the young one I put my hand out to Murray and said, "Mike Brewer." This voice came up from his ankles, and with a super patronising lift of the eyebrow he said, "WHOOOO?"

I said, "Mike Brewer." He went, "MURRAY MEXTED." I said, "How are you, Murray?" I won the toss, and by now I was bloody fuming. Murray said, "What are you going to do, SON?" I was that angry I said, "I'll tell you when we run out." He looked at me a bit harder then, probably thinking, "What have we got here?"

I decided to play into the wind, which would be a real issue after the game. We were down by 26 points at halftime, but came right back in the second half to finally lose 29-24.

After the game Murray came up and said, "Well played, son." I congratulated him on the win and he said, "I think experience told in the end." We talked about the lineouts, where I think we'd won about five each. He basically said I wasn't too bad a jumper. I said, "Thanks, yeah, things were pretty even." Murray said, "Hmmmm…I think I might have got one or two more than you did." How could you not laugh? That's Murray's personality, bigger and bolder than life.

The most notable win we had in '85 was against Auckland. We beat them at Carisbrook 12-10, a week after they won the Ranfurly Shield from Canterbury. Auckland had stayed in the South Island, running their reserves against South Canterbury midweek, then coming to Dunedin. They were stunned when they went down to us, but we closed David Kirk down on the blindside all day, and that was an important part of their play.

It was one of the most enjoyable wins we had on the 'Brook, and it came from a lot of analysis. We'd been watching Auckland all season, and studied the Shield game closely. Basically we devised a plan to beat them, with me standing off on the blindside to stop Kirky. They'd come off the high of a Shield victory, and that was always going to make playing against us hard, but they were a very, very good side, and we were an average side. We won by doing our homework, seeing where Auckland were making their yardage, and closing it down.

Our jubilation over the victory turned to absolute horror straight after the game, when Alan Mills, the president of the Otago union, and a man we all knew and liked, had a heart attack and died in our changing room. The aftermatch function was cancelled as a mark of respect, and none of us felt like celebrating the win privately either.

The Otago union's administrators were a lot more forward thinking that most unions in New Zealand at the time. We had a players' committee of five or six, which would always include a new player, as well as the more senior guys.

Once every two months we'd sit down with two or three delegates from the union's management committee, and the team administration, and discuss everything from discipline to clothing, style of play to sponsorship. They'd say what they wanted from us, and we'd say what we wanted from them.

The union officials were very conscious of the needs of the players, because they realised that with so many students starting to come into the team, they were a wee bit different to the average player. If they don't think they're being properly treated they tend to pack a sad, and not play as well.

It was important for the game in Otago that everyone involved worked together. The image today is that Carisbrook has always had the stands sold out, and a bank full of screaming scarfies as well. That certainly wasn't the case in the early 80s. I remember a game against Wairarapa-Bush in 1983, when I first moved to Dunedin. It was a shocking day, and the game wasn't much better. They drew 15-all, and I swear there wouldn't have been more than 40 of us on the bank. Even for better games there were no more than 4000 people turning up.

The Otago team had to earn their support, and to do that the first need was to start winning. That's why the parameters were so tight in '85 and '86. But we always had goals, and a plan. We knew where we were heading.

* * *

Laurie Mains: Team spirit and loyalty was the real basis on which I developed my coaching. It didn't take Mike long to understand the spirit of what Otago rugby is all about. In those early years the guys put the gold "O" before all else. Certainly a long way before themselves. Mike quickly adopted that philosophy.

He didn't have it all his own way with some people. There were some on the Otago union management committee who asked me if I knew what I was doing making him captain. And while Mike was the golden-haired boy, playing so well, he still had to work hard to be totally accepted.

He got the "Goldenballs" tag for a couple of years from the other players, but really the only people who thought he was getting it a bit too easy too soon were people on the periphery of the team, not from the key players.

I never doubted that no matter what the tempo of first division play, he was always in total control of his thinking. If I had a criticism of Mike as a captain when he began it was that sometimes he would get a bit angry, not out of control, but angry with a referee, or his own players.

The first year Paul Henderson was in the side, in 1987, we played Taranaki up in New Plymouth. Mike had been troubled with injuries, and wasn't fully fit. It was a dirty, wet, miserable day. From the grandstand I saw Mike rip up Paul Henderson.

The way I saw it, the mistake had basically been Mike's. He should have been more assertive and gone for the ball. Paul hesitated because he thought Mike was going for it. A few other players got criticised through the game too, and generally it wasn't one of Mike's better games as captain.

I thought about talking to him on his own, but I decided the other players should know that he wasn't getting it all his own way. I let him have a barrel in front of the whole team, and it was a pretty savage one.

Basically I said there was no need to take out his own frustrations on the other players, and that if he didn't conform he would be the one who wouldn't be there. It's a measure of him that he took it on the chin, and I don't think the issue was ever raised again.

So occasionally I would have strong words with Mike, but that was very rare. On most things I'd put questions to him. Some players you have to keep dependent on you, because they don't have the confidence, or the intelligence, to be decision makers themselves. Whereas right from day one with Mike it was always a case of a suggestion, or question, or encouragement, to make the decisions himself.

*   *   *

Paul Henderson: My first impression of Mike when I went up to Otago was his passion to succeed. He's very much a perfectionist, and he had a totally professional attitude to the game. Over the five years I played with him that approach never wavered, and it rubbed off on the people around him. His attention to detail helped pick up the whole thing.

*   *   *

I detested failure, and I detested mistakes at training. The biggest thing I brought back to Otago when I got in the All Blacks was the attitude the All Blacks had at training.

As a newcomer to the All Blacks you used to actually be scared about going to training. You dreaded doing anything wrong during the drills. That's why the skill level was so high in the All Blacks. If you made a mistake at training the older guys got on your case so badly you looked for a shovel to dig a hole and jump in it. The pressure was incredible, but it also led to competition, and it made us raise our expectations of ourselves.

When I went back to Otago with that philosophy, it was probably hard on some of the players. While that sort of intensity is quite acceptable to international players, some players are quite happy to play provincial rugby. They don't want that extra step up. So I'm sure Steve Cumberland (an experienced prop) used to think I was a grumpy young bastard. It was probably only in the last few years we played together that Cumby understood why I did it.

It's an odd thing about rugby players. If you don't ask for certain levels of intensity and performance they won't give it to you. Give them a structure they have to stay within, they'll perform. If you let them waver outside it, they don't.

Otago were a classic example of that. If Laurie or I weren't on their case, they'd play badly. Then as soon as we got back to the normal routine of hammering them, they'd perform.

As time went by I could see that the Auckland personnel were getting older. Basically they were an era older than we were. So if we kept on performing, we could win the national championship. That meant putting pressure on the players at every training run.

In the end it worked. It became engraved in the guys' psyche. What was expected in training, and what we then took from training onto the field. If you don't give it 100 per cent at training, if you're not used to feeling the hurt, then you stop.

If you stop when you're training, then it's so much easier to stop during a game. In training if you start to ease up you can be screamed at by the guy on the sideline wearing the coach's hat. On the field there's nobody there to point the finger, because everyone else is too busy doing his job.

One thing that Laurie worked on endlessly with Otago, and succeeded in creating, was a great team spirit. If you made comparisons with other provincial sides we didn't have the sheer physical presence, nor the skill, so to match them we had to be fitter, more aggressive, and want it more.

We developed that team culture in many different ways. What

became vital was that we had a vision of where we wanted to be, and worked towards it.

If you only work towards short term goals, you have elements of doubt creep in, you wonder what things will be like in two or three or four years. Things can change, but as long as people know what their roles are, so they're heading in the same direction, people are far happier.

It's like business. If you don't have a job description, you either have to be instructed every day, or you just sit there and get frustrated.

When we sat down to look at the 1988 season, when we'd lost the likes of Ken Bloxham, we sat down and said, "What's it going to take to win the national championship?" We looked at building a team, and developing a style of play to win the championship in 1992.

As players we started to have more of a say in the style being played, and the personnel. Not just myself and Laurie, but with a players' group we'd talk about picking teams for a game.

We actually dropped Dave Latta for a game against Waikato in Hamilton in 1988. Dave had been our hooker right through the season, but we believed that Andrew Roose would scrummage better, and Waikato then had an incredible front row of Richard Loe, Warren Gatland and Graham Purvis.

The plan was to hold them in the tight five, so the loosies would be able to knock them over around the fringes, because basically that was Waikato's game plan, attacking off a powerful tight core. When we announced the team the players were quite shocked. David took it brilliantly, as David would.

We went out on Rugby Park in Hamilton, held them in the tight five, though we were under pressure, kept knocking them over in the loose, and won the game 30-10.

That sort of thing does an enormous amount for a team's spirit. The team had some input in terms of a plan and selection. The unlucky player recognises the needs that led to him being on the bench. And when you implement the game plan, and win, the whole team feel they've done it together.

Then after the games it became a tradition, known throughout the country, that Otago always had their court sessions. Sometimes you could get sick of them, but generally you had a bit of fun, poked some fun at the administration, released the tension, and brought the team closer together.

You do that for a few weeks, picking the team as a team, developing your style of play, implementing it, having success, then having a drink afterwards as a group, enjoying the win together, and it snowballs. The momentum gathers all the time.

So we reached a stage where players put the team before their own egos. You could feel it in the atmosphere when we came together for a training run, even in the off-season. The team just jelled, like brothers who hadn't seen each other for a few years meeting again. We didn't need to spend a lot of time together in the summer, the feeling was there immediately. That's the great beauty of an ego-free climb, there are no undercurrents, no one-upmanship.

We were primed for a breakthrough, and it really came in 1988, when a casual young scarfie called John Timu arrived, and the pieces all fell into place.

In 1987 we'd had a good year in the national championship, finishing in third place, and the forwards were getting more confidence in the backs. JT's brilliance sealed it. There was no use having a guy like him sitting on the wing not getting any ball.

JT came into the side quietly. He kept a pretty low profile, but when he hit the field that was when you saw what he could do in action. In August we had three home games in a row, and JT scored four tries in the first, four in the second, and one in the third. His try against Taranaki really stays in my mind. He just stood up his man so well with an inside-outside that his wing didn't even get a finger on him. I thought, "Jeez, this guy's really got some talent."

It never had any effect on JT. He'd play his game, walk off the field, say "see you later" and get back to scarfieland. He's free and easy, and that lifestyle hasn't changed. I don't think Winfield Cup league will change it either.

*   *   *

Laurie Mains: It was basically a happy coincidence John Timu arriving. In 1988 we had, in Mike, Brent Pope and Paul Henderson, as good a loose forward trio as you could ever hope to get. Then we had Arthur Stone at second-five, and JT and Noel Pilcher, who was in awesome form himself after being out with a knee injury, on the wings.

Because we had loose forwards with real ability to run with the ball we developed a style of play that got them into the game, doing the damage on the opposition. Then, when our backs got the ball, the opposition were usually a man or two down, because they'd had to tackle the Brewers, the Popes, the Hendersons.

It went right back to the start of the '88 season when we went to Australia and thumped the Aussie Barbarians by 20 odd points. Then we went to Australian Capital Territory and put 50 points round them. The loose forwards were just outstanding.

Sure, John Timu was a great finisher, and in the past we maybe hadn't been able to finish well, but the impact of the loose forwards created so many more opportunities for the backs, and the backs came out of their shells. We had limitations in other areas, but we had two or three years from those three loosies that were just magic.

*　　*　　*

When the ball started rolling in '88 the crowds started to get bigger and bigger at Carisbrook, and the scarfies began what would become their fanatical support of the side. People like seeing tries scored, and in '88 a lot of them were being scored by a scarfie, John Timu.

While the results for the season would be best in '91, the year that we really played the best style of rugby while I was in Otago was 1988.

It would have been even better if we'd achieved what was regarded as the impossible, beating Auckland for the Ranfurly Shield. In '88 we came so close.

The biggest barrier when you went to Eden Park to challenge was their tight five. You had to combat them to have a chance of winning. We were really under pressure all day in the tight, but if they tried to move the ball round the fringes, we knocked them over. If they moved it wide, and then used Joe Stanley coming back inside, Brent Pope, Ginge Henderson or I knocked them back before the advantage line.

Thirteen minutes into the second half Noel Pilcher intercepted a pass, and went straight in for a try that gave us a 17-12 lead. A few minutes later he cut through Auckland again, and was sailing towards the goalline. The game was all over. Then Frank Bunce, who had replaced Terry Wright on the wing, came out of nowhere and drilled Noel on the line.

Auckland scrambled out of it, but you could see the look on their faces. They were thinking, "It's gone today."

We had them pinned inside their 22, with our ball to a scrum in a good attacking position, about 20 metres in from the left hand touchline. We won the ball, but there was a breakdown in communications between Popey at No 8 and Shane Stone at halfback. The ball was knocked on.

They got the put-in, kicked downfield and won the lineout. Foxy put an up and under in, and within a couple of minutes they were scrummaging on our line. Zinny Brooke got a pushover try. That was a feature of Auckland then, and in many ways it still is. At Eden Park especially, if they get close to your line, they'll score a try. In '88 our guys had given it everything, but we dropped it. One mistake cost us the shield.

To take the shield you really needed to dominate Auckland in the tight five. We didn't dominate them, yet we nearly won. But nearly isn't good enough. When Waikato finally took the shield, they did dominate the tight play.

Our long term goal in '88 was to win the national championship in 1992, and we actually got there a year earlier. We were helped by the World Cup taking some key players away for the last three games of the competition, when we beat Auckland 17-6 at Carisbrook. But the fact we won nine out of our 10 games in '91 was a tribute to the culture that had developed inside the team.

Laurie worked hard on stamping out egos. We certainly had players with such individual abilities they could have grown away from the team. Players like Greg Cooper, JT, Rhys Ellison, Arthur

Stone, John Haggart, Stu Forster, Ant Strachan, Brent Pope, Gordy Macpherson, Steve Cumberland, Dave Latta and Steve Hotton could all have become individuals, rather than placing the team first.

There were times when some players didn't feel they were getting the accolades they should. You would say that Brent Pope was probably more of an individual than a Dave Latta. When Arran Pene started putting the pressure on Popey at No 8 there were times when the selection would be made on the basis of whether we wanted to play a tighter game, or a wider game. Whenever a decision had to be made it was Laurie who would handle the confrontational stuff.

But if there was a player who felt he hadn't been fairly treated, he would usually come to me, saying "What's the story? Why? Why? Why? I should be playing." Popey was probably the most frequent.

My argument then was that it came down to consistency of performance. If they wanted to be first choice selections every time, or become All Blacks, they had to be consistent. So the way to enhance your own ego was to play well every week, then you'll get picked for the All Blacks, and your team will get the accolades as well.

A prime example would be Paul Henderson. When Ginge played for Otago he actually lived in Invercargill. I believe he had the attitude that there was more chance of him becoming an All Black from Otago than there was if he was playing for Southland. So, if you compared him with an Arran Pene, when Arran started playing for Otago, Ginge was probably playing the game more for himself than for the team.

I see nothing wrong with that. Ginge was a man who set himself very high standards with fitness levels, and that was aimed at becoming an All Black. Ambition rules a move to a province where there's more chance of becoming an international, and that's how it should be. It happened that our style of play really suited him. If he'd played for Otago in the early 80s, when our style was much more restrictive he would have been very frustrated, and probably ended up leaving.

Don't get me wrong. Ginge fitted in superbly, and he was an absolutely integral part of Otago winning the championship in '91. He was definitely one of the best openside flankers in the world. The style of game we played in the late 80s was to put the ball on the ground, and then move it wide. It's a measure of Ginge's ability that I never saw him outplayed by Michael Jones when we played Auckland, and Ginge was operating off a forward pack going backwards. If Ginge had been playing on the side of the Auckland scrum he'd have got the test spots.

Ginge is a man with a very dry sense of humour, and when we were on tour the guys really enjoyed his company. But he's very much a family man, who wanted to spend more time with his family than with the "boys" so to speak. When we played in Dunedin he'd spend the time he had to with the team, then be off for the two hour drive to Invercargill. We were team mates, but we were never close personally. Away from the game we went our own ways.

*   *   *

Paul Henderson: That's a good summation. We were rugby friends, and I enjoyed his company immensely. But it never developed beyond that, perhaps because it was just physically difficult for us to spend much time together with Mike in Dunedin and me in Invercargill.

Some people were surprised that I wasn't at Mike and Bev's wedding, but I wasn't surprised or disappointed at all. We got on well, but people who thought we were like Bernie and Stu were well off the beam. We never spent much time together away from rugby.

*   *   *

Steve Hotton was another very important player to Otago. In some ways Hotty was to the tight five what John Haggart was to the backline. John's tactical sense was a major reason for our success, and Hotty was crucial in letting me know what was really happening up front.

As a loose forward you might think that things are pretty even in the tight five, but they might feel they're starting to get on top. You need to know exactly what's going on. It can be the difference between winning and losing a game. That slight edge the tight five are getting can be lost if you start to spin the ball wide too soon, and allow the game to become fragmented.

Hotty was always regarded as the team clown, the man who helped make up the balance you need. It was in his nature to crack a joke when things were getting too tense, or getting down, and the team would come back up again.

But as much as he was the character, the man with the fan club and the reputation as a joker, he hated losing. He took it as badly as anyone if we lost, and in the heat of game he'd throw his body on the line, and play it right to the limit. He knew everything that was required technically in a front row, and with his experience he knew what was required of individuals.

Hotty always had a lot of ideas away from rugby, and most of them involved him becoming a millionaire as quickly as possible. He was into the hotel business, he was into raising angora goats, he was really something of an entrepreneur. His aim was always to be the first into something new, but so far it seems he's been unlucky enough to be fourth of fifth. Knowing Hotty he'll keep trying until he hits that jackpot.

Gordon Macpherson was the ultimate engine room worker. If you wanted a tight forward to be rock solid physically and mentally, Gordy was the guy I would pick. I don't think I ever played with an international forward that had a more committed attitude to rugby, to competition, to training, than Gordy.

The only thing that kept him from a great test career was that his agility was never of the standard of a true test lock. He didn't have the explosiveness needed to be successful in test lineouts. Perhaps he was just working off too small a platform. For a man as tall as Gordy he had exceptionally small feet, size nine.

But he had amazing strength. Being a carpenter he was immensely strong in the shoulders, the arms, the wrists, the hands. I saw him rip the ball off internationals like they were schoolboys. The only guy that would come close to Gordy's strength in the rucks, mauls and scrums, would be Robin Brooke. But I still don't think Robin has the commitment that Gordy had.

*   *   *

Laurie Mains: One of the things that every rugby follower in Otago would say about Mike: When the chips were down he really gave it everything. He's totally a team man. I believe that if he didn't think he was the right man to play a game, he'd talk himself out of the team. That was the level of his commitment to the team.

8

Loyal

People who have been rubbed up the wrong way by Laurie Mains have to realise that he has a passion for his team to succeed that in my experience is even greater than Grizz Wyllie's or John Hart's.

He has a fanatical loyalty to the team he's coaching, whether it's a club side, Otago, or the All Blacks. In fact, his coaching philosophy as I've observed it, revolves around the team coming first, and the individual components within the team having to fit in with what the team needs.

Laurie wants to get to know his players, how they react, how they prepare, those who struggle to deal with pressure. He'll talk to players individually before a game, then with the groups inside the team, like inside backs and the loosies. Then, when he believes he's done as much as he can, he just watches and observes.

Once he knows his players, he certainly has the ability to judge who he needs to leave alone to prepare in their own way, and who he needs to have a crack at, even in front of the team. He doesn't let an individual's pride take precedence over what's best for the team.

But he has never been a coach to play mind games with players. In his book, *"Fronting Up"*, Sean Fitzpatrick says that John Hart "manipulates players very cleverly. It's effective, but not a very comfortable experience. When I was playing for Auckland I know

Abo (Iain Abercrombie the other Auckland hooker) felt the same way because we'd discuss it. Harty would say something to Abo, and then he would say something else to me. We'd find out there were two different versions by comparing stories."

By contrast look at what happened in Otago with two men competing for the one spot, Brent Pope and Arran Pene. When Popey was on song he was, I believe, as good a No 8 as Buck Shelford. But at times Popey would lose a bit of form, and have a couple of bad games. At those times, as the younger player, Arran would upset the incumbent, Popey. But basically it was known to the team, and to them, that Popey was No 1 and Arran was No 2. Arran got the games when Popey was off song. Laurie never played one off against the other.

Laurie Mains: Brent Pope was a great mate of Mike's. Mike had a lot of respect for him as a player, and so did I. But here was the difference between Mike and Popey. Right from the early days Mike was never afraid to say what he felt. If he thought I was wrong, he'd tell me. Mike was never afraid to confront me, or to confront another player. Popey was never one to come to me if he had a grizzle. He'd tell someone else, usually Mike. From time to time Mike would come to me and say, "Have a yarn with this guy, he's pissed off about something that's happened." I never minded a guy who put me on the mat. How am I going to improve if the players don't keep me honest? Even with the All Blacks, in '92, Mike had great difficulty convincing the players who didn't know me that I welcomed them coming and confronting me on issues that upset them. From the time Mike was just a boy he was open and up front, which made it very easy to work with him. There was never anything simmering under the surface.

* * *

Harty's style, of virtually fermenting competition between players, can work well when you've got a group of players who are skilled to a level that is better than any other team in the country. But if you try to play those mental games with players of lesser ability, all you'll do is wreck their confidence. If Harty did it with the current All Black side, for example, he'd blow the team to bits.

Laurie's attitude with Otago was based on loyalty to players. His loyalty was one of the reasons for the success of Otago when he was the coach. He made sure you kept performing at training and on the paddock, but if you put the work in, you basically knew you would keep the spot.

That gave players the confidence to go out and play their natural game. In 1994 Laurie moved away from that a bit with the All Blacks. The national pressures from the media and the public after losing a few test matches had an effect.

Laurie hasn't always been treated well by the media, which probably dates back to when he was first coaching Otago. We were a middle of the road national championship side, striving to be something more.

His aim was to get the side to the top, and he did that. Along the way he created a bit of a protective environment. Usually the media didn't really hone in on Otago until we were about to challenge for the Ranfurly Shield.

I think his mentality was that we were usually not as talented and skilled as a lot of the sides we were playing against, so he didn't want outside pressures that would take away the focus we needed so much. Hopefully, the media would move on to our opposition.

In the north one of the lingering images of Laurie is of him running to a fence, telling a camera crew we were having a private training run before a shield challenge.

The impression created of Laurie wasn't great, but the reality was that teams do have certain moves they keep up their sleeve for special matches. In years past, teams have been known to sneak a spy into the opposition's training runs to check out such moves.

Today, if you allow unhindered access to television crews, they're not going to differentiate between the footage, and cut out what might be the move you're going to use in the match to win the game.

Having said that, Laurie has had to change with the times with the All Blacks. Television is such an important marketing tool for rugby that you must make the effort to accommodate them, and I believe Laurie's done that. In 1994, when he was under quite bitter attack from the electronic media, he was prepared to front up for the Holmes show, knowing there was likely to be a grilling in store for him.

It would be fantastic for Laurie, and for myself, because I carry some similar feelings towards the media to him, to be able to sit down with the journalists at the start of the season, and go through the objectives and the goals you have for your team.

If you could explain the style you were trying to evolve for the whole season, then a journalist could take a much more in-depth look at each game. Instead of just writing, or broadcasting, about what happened on the day they could see whether the team was on track, which is probably more newsworthy than just passing an opinion on a game many people will have seen on television for themselves.

The problem is that there's a feeling, which I might have if I was a coach, that some of the journalists in New Zealand, if they felt they had the jewel from some confidential background information, would let the cat out of the bag.

Trust is built up between some teams or players and journalists, but the feeling remains that with some journalists the urge to make a quick name for themselves would outweigh everything else. It's short-term thinking on their part, but it does happen.

My own relationship with Laurie certainly rests very heavily on trust. Not once since the first day I met him have I ever seen him behave without integrity and honesty.

Having said that, it might be a surprise for people when I say that Laurie and I don't have a close personal relationship. If I was visiting Dunedin tomorrow the first thing in my mind wouldn't be to call Laurie and arrange to have a drink with him.

I respect him, and do enjoy his company, but right from the start Laurie was never one of the boys with Otago. He mixed with the guys after the games, joined in our court sessions and drinks, and went to the Shoreline for dinner on game nights, but outside of that direct Otago rugby environment there wasn't a lot of contact.

In many ways, I'd call our relationship a business one. When

I was in Dunedin, if Laurie called me it wouldn't be to say, "What are you and Bev doing in the weekend? Let's get together for a meal." Whenever I got a phone call it was to talk about tactics, players, opposing teams, the business side of the game.

*   *   *

Laurie Mains: I really like Mike as a person, and I have a great deal of respect for his ability, not just in rugby, but in other things. He'll mix it at any level, and he's dead straight.

I enjoy having a beer with him, but even when he lived in Dunedin, I wouldn't have kept in touch with him any more than I do now he's in Christchurch, and at times a month or more can go by without us talking. I'm not really one for idle chit chat, and Mike's much the same. That's just how it is. If there's nothing constructive to say, don't talk about it.

There wasn't a need for a lot of talk even when Mike was the Otago captain and I was the coach. Because there's no bullshit between us we might have five minutes before training, and about three times in a whole season he'd come and see me at work to talk something through.

Only once did we have harsh words with each other. We'd played a game against Southland, in Invercargill, on a dirty, rotten day when it was actually snowing. Because of road safety we decided we wouldn't go back to Dunedin on the bus that night.

Mike and a few of the others decided they'd go straight from Invercargill to Queenstown the next day for a bit of skiing, then go back to Dunedin. I killed it.

My reasoning was that we were in the middle of the provincial season, and these guys had a responsibility, not just to the other players in the team, but to the management, and to the Otago Rugby Union who were spending so much money on them, and relied on them so much. It was wrong to take the risk of injuring themselves in such a high risk sport.

With half a dozen of them going, the chances of losing somebody for the following Saturday was pretty high. Some of them weren't great skiers. But you couldn't say to some, "You can go," and tell others they couldn't.

The next day it was obvious to me that Mike was very angry

about it. So I went and sat next to him in the bus, and let him get it off his chest, and he did.

He told me that rugby was not his only priority in life, and he didn't see why he shouldn't go skiing. I told him my reasons, and that was the end of it. It was a little bit more of getting to know each other. I'd be surprised now if he'd want to take a risk like that in the middle of a first division season.

*　　*　　*

Laurie will always confront a problem. If there's a tiff in the side he likes to get it out in the open, whether it's a screaming match, or just a pointed discussion, he wants it resolved.

One of the reasons we got on so well together in Otago was that Laurie puts such a lot of thought into his own side, and a hell of a lot of thought into the opposition side, to the point where you'll slightly digress from your normal game plan to expose weaknesses of the opposition, or to deal with one of their strengths.

He's very analytical about each game as it comes along. I like to try to be as analytical as possible about each game too, both before and after the match, working out why some things worked and some things didn't.

Laurie and I would bounce a lot of ideas off each other, blindside moves, defensive screens, lineout variations. I find it interesting, and it's also rather like a case study for a lawyer. The background reading you do can be the nail in the coffin for a case. Likewise the study you make of the opposition can be the difference between winning and losing.

The game has become more sophisticated in the 1990s, but in the '80s a lot of teams just went out and worked and worked on what they wanted to do. They didn't really look at what the opposition was going to be doing. That was where we were able to shut down teams.

Our 1985 win over Auckland at Carisbrook, 12-10, was the classic example of planning paying off. The blindside was where Auckland made most of their yardage on the paddock. Man for man they were a very good side, while we were an average side. But we'd done the homework, analysed it, and closed them down where they were usually the most potent. It was the planning, and the fact it paid off, that made the victory so enjoyable.

From the early days with Otago, Laurie would call me and pose questions. "This is what Auckland are doing. This is what Canterbury are doing. What can we do to counter it?" His knowledge and understanding of the game had pinpointed what the opposition were doing, and what we were trying to do. He'd run it out for me, then I'd go away, and usually look at a video of the opposition.

When we got back together again we'd bounce ideas off each other, and between the two of us we'd get the chemistry right more often than not.

*   *   *

Laurie Mains: I got into the habit of really working at tactics to counter specific teams when I took over coaching my club. I was a brash young man, just out of 10 years in first division provincial rugby, and I looked round the club scene, and reckoned I could work out tactics to bowl the other teams.

At the start of the year, with the players we had, people said we wouldn't make the top six, but we went on to win the championship. I knew we didn't have a very talented side, so I had to get into tactics. It was just the same when I took over Otago.

I guess if I've achieved one thing with Mike, and he may have had it when I got hold of him, I'd like to think I've had some influence on his ability to think the game through. I attempted to mould him as a captain by making him do the analysis, and make decisions for himself. He's taken that on to a huge extent.

By comparison a lot of players have virtually been yes-men in their provinces. Look at Olo Brown for example. I spent the first two years with Olo in the All Blacks trying to draw comment from him.

For so long he'd played for Auckland with their big guns, and I think he was hardly allowed to handle the ball. His job was to scrum, ruck, block in the lineout, and the plums were for the McDowells and the Whettons. Having had a leadership role since he was 20, Mike's moved miles away from that.

As time's gone by, Mike has moved so far ahead of other players in his ability to understand the game that it embarrasses me at times. He has the mental ability to see a defensive pattern, to see in his mind's eye all 30 players on the field, and in a flash see exactly how it's going to work.

At times in team meetings he wants to get into a depth of tactics that I know is just going to confuse other players in the team. He can handle it, but it's too complicated for other players to see it. I know he gets a bit frustrated about it, but at times I don't want him to go on. I want him back at a level that the other players can handle.

It's not that he's trying to take someone down to bolster himself, or having a crack at somebody. He's entirely genuine in what he's trying to do.

*   *   *

There are no real surprises with how Laurie acts as a coach. Some guys will suddenly jump ship on an idea, or a philosophy, but with Laurie you pretty much knew when you were going to get a hammering.

One thing that has changed a bit from the Otago days is that Laurie has become a bit more expressive when it comes to accolades. He's always been very emotional when there was something going wrong, but when it came to congratulations he's more of the "good on you mate" school.

Grizz Wyllie was much the same. Grizz had a huge vocabulary when it was time to bawl players out, but when it came to praise it was more like, "Yeah (rumble, rumble), keep playing like that, (rumble, rumble), we'll be all right."

In the past with Laurie you had to read it in the way he shook hands, or by the look in his eyes. More recently, with the All Blacks, he has moved on to hugging on occasions. It's pretty much a generational thing in New Zealand, and Laurie's from the non-demonstrative generation.

*   *   *

Laurie Mains: There was one thing about Mike when he was Otago captain that always fascinated me, but I trusted him enough to know that he had his own good reasons for it to never ask him why he did it.

When Mike was injured, you didn't see him at training. If he couldn't give it 100 per cent you wouldn't see him at all. He'd be training on his own, but if he was going to be out for a month, you wouldn't see him, except at the games, for three weeks.

I don't think there would be many provincial captains, or senior players, who could have stayed right away from a team when they were injured. I think there would have been a number of reasons. He trusted us to do it right. He wouldn't want to be at training, taking it easy and not giving it 100 per cent, and he wouldn't want to be shadowing Richard Knight, who was usually captaining the side if Mike was injured.

I was tempted a couple of times to say to Mike, "The guys would like to see you round, to hear another voice from someone who's watching the games, and knows what we're trying to achieve." I was tempted, but I respected his reasons, which I knew would be very good ones. I'm sure he weighed it up, and decided there were more negatives in being there than in being away.

*　　*　　*

Trust is a very big part of my relationship with Laurie, and he is a man I absolutely trust 100 per cent. I've compared our situation to a close business relationship, and that's true. But there is more to it. Usually, if your dealings with another person revolve around business, there are personal friends you'd trust more.

But Laurie is an exception to that rule. Having got to know him as a coach, I've seen him have to make some tough calls, when players have been dropped, and been hurt by it. He was still very, very loyal. In fact, if you could sum him up in one word, from my dealings with him that word would be loyal.

9

Signing the Covenant

In his own quiet way Graeme Bachop can be very persuasive. When Grizz Wyllie was coaching the All Blacks Graeme, with Grizz's encouragement, almost got me to move from Dunedin.

At the time I stayed in Otago, and when I finally did move to Christchurch, in 1992, it was strictly for business reasons. On the All Blacks tour to Australia earlier that year I'd been asked if I wanted to work for Canterbury International. Back home from Australia they offered me a job (largely in the sponsorship area) that Wayne Smith was going to take before he went to Italy to coach Benetton.

That role didn't really interest me, but, after some negotiation, a much broader marketing position with Canterbury International was worked out, and in September of 1992 Bev and I shifted to Christchurch. I played the last few games for Otago in 1992 while living in Canterbury.

There seemed little chance that I'd play rugby in 1993. Canterbury International went through a major restructuring in '92, and it would really have been impossible to do justice to the job, train, and play football at the same time.

It was always in my mind to play the '94 season in the hope of making the World Cup in '95. I never retired, although that seemed to be the impression some journalists had.

Work was taking up six-and-a-half days a week at the start of the winter of '93, and driving a desk did nothing for my physical condition. From a playing weight of around 100kg I ballooned up to 110kg. Training was virtually impossible. I watched a couple of club games, and the same number of provincial games. Work was so all consuming there was little time to pay attention to anything else.

It must have been late in July when Graeme Bachop asked if I'd be interested in playing the last three games of the '93 season for Canterbury, because their regular flanker, Greg Smith, had taken up an offer to play in Japan, and he was leaving at the end of August.

I talked about it with Bev and some friends, and they all said it was stupid, that I'd just be setting myself up. Canterbury hadn't really been performing, and the rest of the players in first division had been through six months of hard football.

Why did I still decide to play? Grim (Graeme Bachop) being a good mate was probably the main reason, it was also a challenge, and at the back of my mind was the thought that it was just a little payback for not coming to Canterbury a few years earlier. When the Canterbury coach, Vance Stewart, made the formal invitation to join the squad my mind was already made up.

At training my first impressions weren't good. The whole environment, it seemed to me, was ripe for a team to fail. Ill discipline was rife.

Midweek training was always due to start at 6pm. I was having to leave work a lot earlier than usual to make the start time, but then we all had to wait while some players rolled in at 10 past six, even quarter past six.

That lack of commitment to the team at training carried through onto the field. Guys gave away penalties when they didn't have to, they got offside, they dropped passes, they missed tackles. There seemed to be no rules, and no disciplines to meet. Trainings dragged out, and we'd do a lot of talking, without much real pressure on the players to perform. Even in the warmups there would be dropped passes. The skill level was appalling.

My first game for Canterbury was against, of all teams, Otago, at, of all places, Carisbrook. I remembered, only too clearly, that when I was the Otago captain and somebody like Rhys Ellison, who had left Otago to go to the Waikato, came back to the 'Brook, making a point of saying, "Make sure they know they've been in a game." I'm sure the same word went out from Arran Pene before we went on the field.

It was a very tough game, but we were in the match with 25 minutes to go. At that point Canterbury's lack of fitness, and ample self doubt, came into play. Otago blew us away, and won by 30 points.

We came back to Lancaster Park, beat Taranaki, and then faced Wellington at home in a game that would decide whether Canterbury would finish near the top four, or near the bottom, of the first division. After the Taranaki game my input was mainly to suggest we develop some home ground pride. We battled to do it, but we beat Wellington, 15-12, and generally I'd really enjoyed my short, sharp, 1993 season.

At the end of the '93 season Vance said to me fairly casually, "If you're going to play next year, I'd really like you to be the Canterbury captain."

I said, "What about Rob Penney (the captain in '93). Is he pulling the pin?"

Vance said, "No, I've made the decision that Rob'll be part of the squad if he's playing well enough, but I want you to captain the team."

*   *   *

Vance Stewart: It wasn't that hard a decision for me to make, although I knew it could have gone down pretty poorly in Canterbury. Mike's just a natural leader. It was commonsense to make him captain.

*   *   *

I agreed, as long as Vance talked it over with the senior players, like Grim, Shayne Philpott, Matt Sexton and Rob himself. Vance said that was fine.

From my experience with Otago I didn't expect any announcement until the following February. So in November, when I was sitting in a hotel in Edinburgh, working for Canterbury International as their representative with the All

Blacks, it was a real surprise to get a phone call from Bob Schumacher, the rugby reporter for The Press in Christchurch.

"Congratulations," said Bob, "you've just been appointed Canterbury captain."

I said, "Hell, I didn't even know anything about it." And I didn't.

As it turned out, European travel had made it difficult for Vance to get in touch with Rob Penney. Rob had gone to Italy, and while Vance had talked with several other senior players who were more than happy for me to be captain, he hadn't had the chance to talk to Rob face to face. So he hadn't had a really good chat with Rob to the level I would have liked.

I suppose it was inevitable there would be some negative reaction to a former Otago player who comes to Christchurch, might appear to have not had the interest to play through 1993, had a few games, and the next minute is captain. It's even worse when he replaces a captain who has led the side through several previous seasons.

* * *

Vance Stewart: Some people probably saw it as a person coming from outside the province and, in a limited time, taking over from Rob Penney. But there was never a question over whether Mike should be captain. There was never a question of whether it was acceptable to the team. It was only the wider Canterbury rugby community who initially saw it as a negative thing.

* * *

Inside the team I was well aware that some cliques could be a concern. Burnside, as one of the more powerful clubs in the city, had a strong representation in the side, and as their captain at club level, Rob was very much the Pied Piper to them. He's a very strong personality, and as far as the Burnside players went, what he says goes.

Everything was fine for the first couple of games, but as soon as Rob came back from Italy the Burnside boys, in particular, were straight back together as a group beside him. They were covering their own butts in a way. Not that Rob was trying to cause any disruption when he returned, he actually accepted the whole situation very well. But he has a strong influence within the team, as I have I suppose, and the change of leadership took some adjustments for some of the players.

There was never a need for anything drastic or dramatic to happen. As the side got more and more successful any divisions just dissipated. By the time we got to the business end of the season everything was fine.

*   *   *

Vance Stewart: Shayne Philpott was always the one who was really sitting there, waiting for something to happen. It did take some time to dissipate, but it's certainly run its course now.

We did have a lot of newer players who had not come through in the team with Rob. So young players like Andrew Mehrtens, who would follow Mike over a cliff, got in behind and followed him. So Mike had the majority with him, and the covenant helped deal with any doubters too.

Rob himself is loyal to Canterbury rugby, and there was never going to be a problem with him being a disruptive influence. I was confident about that. He's a bloke who gives it 110 per cent, and for all his rough edges, he's really likeable. Nothing was going to change his attitude to the team.

*   *   *

Taking on the captaincy of Canterbury was largely because I saw huge potential in the team, probably more raw talent than we'd had in Otago. Having been through the experience of team building in Otago I knew we could do it a lot more quickly in Canterbury.

It was a matter of working with Vance and the other guys to harness that talent by pointing the individuals in the team in the right direction. I thought that if I didn't have the captaincy I might be seen as intruding on the territory of whoever was the captain. As a captain you can sculpture the team as quickly as you like.

The change of environment, with new management, new voices, new coaching styles, new skills and drills was also quite refreshing. It put a bounce into your step.

131

Right from the start I sat down with Vance and the senior players, and we talked about what was needed to get the players aerobically fit. At that stage they were running with sleds, and power and sprint work.

But they ran out of steam with 30 minutes to go. They could be relatively competitive until the last quarter, and then they got rolled over by fitter teams. I'd been through it all with the All Blacks, and saw what happened at the '91 World Cup to them.

So when we sat down to look at the season I said, "You can do all the sprint stuff, but do it after you've done the hard work, the aerobic running." We agreed that the first thing the players could do was to put some miles in their legs and their lungs. They could do that in their own time over summer. Later we met out at the Burwood forest, and when we ran through there it was obvious the players had put the work in and were looking pretty good as far as aerobic fitness was concerned.

A prime example was Grant Kelly, "Ned" to the team because of his surname, the big lock. In the Waikato he'd been a player on the way up, but in Christchurch he was carrying too much puppy fat. I said to Ned, "You've got to get out there and start doing the miles over summer."

Just after Christmas I saw him, and he was in superb shape. He'd lost all the fat by doing the miles, and began the club season as the No. 1 lock, because he was in such good shape. His early season form was good enough to get him into the New Zealand Maori team, but then he got a couple of niggly injuries, got a bit down in the dumps, and lost his way a little.

He was coming right near the end of the '94 season, and had a very good shield challenge in Hamilton. It would have been good to spend more time with Ned individually, but the biggest problem I've had as Canterbury captain is that with my job commitments I can't work individually with players as much as would be ideal.

Vance and I sat down once to look at what we wanted to do for the whole season, deciding on a squad of 26, and discussing our goals and objectives. Then we had a team meeting on the first available Sunday we could all get together in the New Year.

We met at Rugby Park, and I didn't say a thing at the start, when the players discussed the strengths and weaknesses of the Canterbury side.

One would say we had good loose forwards, another that we had a good front row, we had good kickers, a strong midfield, in fact, apart from a few weaknesses in tackling, we were superb in almost every area. Then it was my turn to speak.

"I would say that the greatest weakness in this team is a lack of honesty." They stopped in their tracks.

"You've got to be honest with yourself, and honest with each other. Until you get that you won't have any success at all.

"Look at the strengths you say we have. Your area of strength is the whole team, right through to the reserves. That's just not true. We've got some glaring weaknesses.

"We do have some strengths, but not if you compare them with the very best first division sides."

There was some more discussion, a few laughs, and then they saw what's probably the harder side of me within the team environment.

"Unless you have honesty with yourself and your team-mates, I'm not even interested in you as a player."

From there we all knew what the rules were, that if you weren't digging it in, you weren't going to be involved. We talked about the games that we were placing the emphasis on for the season, and how the players would have to peak to meet those priorities. We talked how some players who would have All Black trials, and possibly test matches, would have to create their own peaks and troughs.

We took about three hours that Sunday, but it was really essential so that everyone knew where we were heading.

A covenant was formed about disciplines, punctuality, the effort at training. It was agreed that if you were late for training more than twice, you were out of the side. At training you compete with yourself to get through with the least number of mistakes. As training becomes better, you play better, and there's a lot more competition within the squad. That can be damaging if you have the wrong mix of people, but with the right attitude the results keep getting better and better.

The covenant covered the effort on the field, and the effort off it, for sponsorship and promotion. The whole thing ended up being a commitment to the team, not to yourself. We walked out with the season mapped out ahead of us, and I think that session ended up setting us away for the year.

*   *   *

Todd Blackadder: The discipline that Mike demanded, at training and in a game, was a lot higher than we'd had previously. I can tell you that he's not backward in coming forward if there are mistakes being made. There are no shortcuts with Mike. The honesty factor is always there. You can't hide behind the curtain.

The discipline that Mike instilled, and the way he ran the game made it so much easier for me to play my game. His leadership qualities are outstanding. I've never been captained by anybody like it. He's got a mana about him, Mike Brewer. I think he has anyway.

When he retires from football I think he'll be an awesome coach one day, as high as he wants to go. He knows his rugby. I hope his football career isn't over when he stops actually playing.

*   *   *

Vance Stewart: The covenant was something of a flow through from the previous years when things hadn't been going well. I wouldn't say there was dissent within the team, but within the Canterbury rugby community there was dissent over who was being selected, and who wasn't being selected. Some of the reserves were going to their club representatives on the union, and they were having a go there. Things were being slipped to the media that should have been kept in-house. So, to a degree, we were beating ourselves to death.

So we sat down and really talked along a theme that I think Benjamin Franklin said when signing the American Declaration of Independence, "We shall all hang together, least we all hang separately."

We looked at the whole season, set our goals. Decided what we needed in place with the manager to make everything tick over smoothly, what were the coach's responsibilities, the assistant coach's duties, the masseur's role. We put all that in place.

Then we decided that we'd be loyal to each other. That no matter what happened we wouldn't go sniping at each other in public, through the media. That formed the basis of the covenant.

We had a meeting of the senior players, they all had their ideas, I put it in writing, Mike read it and agreed with what was said. Then we all signed it. It was actually a secret document. Even some officials of the Canterbury union haven't read it. It was a personal thing within the team.

If people didn't want to sign it, then they weren't in the team. They were either with us or against us. It was really good because we committed to each other.

*   *   *

We basically split the winter into mini-seasons, and the first three games were against the Sassanachs (Otago under another name), New South Wales and Wellington. We had a couple of players missing, but Richard Loe was there in the front row, and that gave us some grit in the tight five that had been missing in previous years.

When I was in Otago and we had to play Canterbury we always targeted the tight five, and then the midfield. We knew that if we could get on top of Canterbury in the tight five, then they'd start to go backwards a bit, and the holes would open up in midfield.

Once we started to get some solidity in the tight five, I knew we could have not a bad side. It began at training, we'd warm up well, split into the units, and when we joined together, things were pretty slick. The error rate was pretty low. From the start I'd hammered into the guys that we couldn't afford errors at training, because we'd just take them into the game.

We couldn't read much into the Sassanachs game. Our forwards went well, but Otago were fielding almost a whole new backline. We won 55-31. We beat New South Wales 33-3 on a shocking, wet day. They fielded the best side they could at the time, but had a lot of players out with injuries. The score wasn't really important. What mattered then was the error rate being so low, and the way the forwards ran and passed to each other, dealing with the hand to hand stuff. Near the end of the game Scotty England and Mark McAtamney ran 30 metres or so for Mark to score. That had nothing to do with speedwork, but a lot to do with guts and strength.

The game that really made me start to feel quietly confident was the match with Wellington. They came out and hit us with everything in the first 10 minutes, and quickly ran up a 10 point lead. But whereas the previous year they might have chucked it in, there was a real feeling of confidence in the Canterbury team. They didn't panic at all. We slowly matched them in the forwards, then started dominating them. We won 31-20.

The next mini-season led into the tour match against South Africa. By now I was starting to get to grips with the big change in the Canterbury environment from Otago and the All Blacks.

Things were so much less structured than what I was used to, I actually had some difficulties getting to grips with it. With the All Blacks, when a guy like Foxy was running it, you knew exactly what was going to happen when the ball went out into the backline. You knew what move was on, and who was going to handle it.

Foxy was that precise with his communication that there were actually calls, not just from set pieces, but from rucks and mauls. We created that sort of culture in Otago too, so things were very structured.

With the Canterbury team we had moves from scrums and lineouts, but from second phase, anything goes. There were no rules. Mehrts, or whoever was playing first-five or halfback, could do whatever they wanted to, whether it was moving it wide or chipping it through.

As loose forwards we just had to rove, and make sure we got there when it was needed. With players like Foxy and John Haggart, from Otago, they'd make a call, and you could take off and go to where the move was heading. Now we had to sort of hover, see what was eventuating, and then go.

At times, with Mehrts, Bubs Mayerhofler and Tabai Matson, I think they weren't sure what was going to happen next either. But as long as the loosies were there as a trio, you could handle it. It was a big change for me.

* * *

Vance Stewart: I used to tease Mike when he first came into the team that we'd need some Speights to go with the Canterbury Draught, just for him. He was very loyal to Otago. You couldn't really say anything in the early days that was in any way critical of Otago players. He was very sensitive to that.

The way we played had to be different from the way the All Blacks played. We had to be a bit more expansive than the All Blacks. We want to have a go, push it. In the end we had no trouble at all. He adjusted to it.

* * *

Our last game before playing South Africa was against Southland, and by now the midfield was settled with Mehrts at first-five, Bubs at second-five and Tabs at centre. We'd tried Mark (Mayerhofler) at centre, but it didn't work at all.

Vance told them that if they performed against Southland they'd have the job for the South African game, and the rest of the season. It was important to give them the confidence to play consistently.

So we went down to Invercargill, and Southland aren't an easy team to beat on their home field. The 3Ms played very well, and it was decided that in the game against the Springboks they were to play exactly the kind of adventuresome game they'd played against Southland.

Our main priorities for the rest of the season were to be unbeaten at home, to win the Ranfurly Shield, and to be in the top four in the national provincial competition. The only priority the South African game had was that it fitted in with being unbeaten at home.

I saw the South African game as a good learning experience for the three guys. I didn't think they'd be able to play the style of game they showed at Invercargill against an international side. They wouldn't be given the luxury of time they had been against Southland.

So they went out on Lancaster Park, which was pretty wet and a bit muddy, and they tried their moves. When they didn't work, nobody got frustrated. I just let them go. If it had been a test match I would have called for different moves, but really we were just setting it up for the Ranfurly Shield challenge.

After the game the inside backs got roasted, but not by the team. If you've got young players who are very impressionable, you can't hammer them for trying something that doesn't come off, the way you might with Grant Fox, or Joe Stanley or John Kirwan.

If you hammer them for mistakes when they're trying a move, you stamp the flair out of them. If you look at a guy like Walter Little, that probably happened to him over the last few years. He had a lot of flair and talent, but because the All Blacks were playing such a structured game he lost the ability to show his wares.

In the second half of the Bledisloe Cup in '94 he just played his natural game, and immediately started cutting the line. We haven't had a second-five who could break the line like that since John Schuster went to league.

The Springbok game was also a good, pressure cooker lesson for the Canterbury forwards. When the game began, they didn't attack the Boks the way they would have taken on a first division side. As the game went on they realised that if you play against a decent side, and let them play their game the way they want to, they're difficult to contain. So we were a bit tentative at the start, and by the time we got a roll on towards the end, it was too late.

We weren't disappointed at all after the game though, and we went into the Ranfurly Shield challenge against Waikato with the midfield backs very relaxed. They knew they could try some moves, and if they didn't come off, we'd try something else.

There was a real air of confidence in the Canterbury team heading for the challenge in Hamilton. Waikato weren't going too well, and a bit of steel was coming into our team. It began right in the front row with Richard Loe. In the middle of your tight five he's like a big steel girder. Having him packing down against his old forward pack was a huge psychological boost for us.

At the Tuesday training we tried a little bit too hard, and a few passes went down when guys were rushing and grabbing for the ball. On the Thursday we just eased into the training a bit slower, and ran as a team for quite a long time. Things went very well. We kept everything as low key as we could, just making sure that everyone knew exactly what their roles were.

I had an odd thing happen just before we left Christchurch. A large envelope that looked as if it had come from a child arrived with a local sports newspaper inside, and obscene words scrawled over my picture. Thankfully it was in complete contrast to the attitude of so many Canterbury rugby supporters when we returned from the Waikato.

We flew to Hamilton on Friday, and went to Rugby Park. We didn't have a run there, just allowed the guys to get the feel of the ground. By this stage I knew how the individuals prepared for a game. You could see the range at Rugby Park that afternoon.

Some of the younger guys like Ivan Morgan, Andrew Elvidge and Mark Hammett played hackey sack. Tabai Matson and Mehrts, who had a few kicks that day, were very relaxed too. Graeme Bachop can get quite intense, but usually plays best when he's a bit carefree going into the game. Some players like to be on their own with their thoughts. Todd Blackadder is very focused, and Paula Bale gets hyped up. It's easy to see that Paula is churning away, while with Richard Loe the intensity isn't so obvious, but it's certainly there. Loey and Paula just wandered around by themselves.

Our motel was walking distance from the ground, and we went back for a team meeting that got pretty emotional. They say rugby players don't cry, but that's only in public. After the meeting and a meal we all seemed to drift into the rubber's room. Everyone just wanted to be together. By 11 o'clock the guys had mostly filtered away.

When I woke up on Saturday morning I felt very, very confident. I knew we were going to win enough ball, that we were going to scrum well, and that we were going to force our game onto them.

*   *   *

Vance Stewart: Grizz Wyllie sent a fax from South Africa to

the team room in Hamilton, and he sent it to Mike personally. He wished him the best of luck for the game, and then Grizz wrote in bold letters, "Remember - ATTACK, ATTACK, ATTACK!" It couldn't have been more appropriate. Grizz knew what it was about. Playing Ranfurly Shield rugby is slightly different. You have to seize the initiative.

*   *   *

We got a good start against Waikato, and after 15 minutes I knew we were never going to get beaten. Our whole emphasis that day was on going forward. Even running in support we went forward in the hope play would come up to us if need be, before we went back.

It was following that plan that led to a try for me, set up by Mark Mayerhofler. Technically Mark is a very good second-five, who I believe could develop very much into a Warwick Taylor. He's a good tackler, has a good wiper's punt on him, and in the first 30 metres he's one of the quickest guys in the country. If he works on his right foot kicking, and his sustainable speed he'll be pretty much the complete second-five.

When Mark does make a break, he angles out towards his outsides, as a good second-five should. When he broke against Waikato he was challenged by their fullback Todd Miller, who got square on Mark, figuring that Mark was going to head off to the left, openside, touch. But Mark stepped off his left foot to beat Miller. I was running off the blindside of the scrum, down the right hand side of the field. When Mark stepped off his left foot, he was coming back towards me. He threw a long pass, and I was in the right place at the right time. It had really just been a case of keeping my lines.

My emotions when the game finished, Canterbury winning 29-26, were different from what they would have been if I'd been leading an Otago team. There was a lot of satisfaction from the victory, from how we'd planned our season, structured the peaks, brought in the right guys at the right time, and performed just how we wanted to perform on the day. The way the forwards held up, the way Simon Forrest hit the backline, everything just came off. I was very pleased for the young guys in the team, after being a bit of an also-ran side in '93, they'd made a commitment to the rest of the side, to each other, and they'd had an early reward. They'd won the hardest trophy to get hold of in New Zealand rugby.

I was more than happy that we'd won the shield, but being absolutely honest, it would have stirred more personal emotion if it had been with the players in Otago who I'd shared several years of hard work and disappointments with. On the other hand, Canterbury supporters, the most parochial in the country, had been waiting for a long, long time for the Log to come back to Christchurch. On Sunday morning when we flew in, we expected a couple of hundred, maybe even 500 people to be at the airport.

But to go on to the steps outside the plane, and see the top of the terminal packed, with about 4000 people there all told, was incredible.

With hindsight, I think the air of confidence we'd been building inside the team was also developing with the public. They'd seen from the start of the season how the side was getting better and better. Household names were quickly developing. And the players seen as the stars, the Blackadders, the Merhtens and the Matsons, were the ones who performed in Hamilton.

People got excited about the side, and how the younger guys were going, and that confidence was rewarded. It wasn't as if we'd ground out a win, forwards running off the side of a maul, and peeling over the line. Paula Bale ran in a very good try in Hamilton, and on Moro Sports Extra they named Forrey's try the best of the season.

The tide of support was starting to roll in Canterbury, and it was in full flight when we faced the first challenge, against Counties. We thought we'd get 15,000 people there. At kickoff there was still a stream of people coming into the ground, and 20 minutes of the game had gone before an amazing 30,000 people had found seats. On the field we could feel the atmosphere, which was actually better than for the first French test earlier in the season. If you'd played in both it was quite incredible, and yet another sign of how fanatical Canterbury's rugby fans are.

In that environment the start of the Counties game felt very much like a test, and I could actually feel how the Canterbury team were getting better and better at handling it. They were actually better at coping with an electric atmosphere than the All Blacks were in '94. Canterbury would get the ball early on, and attack one area of the opposition, whether it was a high kick into the box, a wipers, or an attack in the midfield. They'd attack the one area, and whoof, everyone would be there, going for the jugular.

It was the way that Canterbury, when they had the shield in the '80s, and Auckland, during their record reign, played the game. They were very, very methodical early in the match. Target the area, put the ball there, blow everything out of the way, and either win the ball and score, or force the other side to infringe. Then Foxy (in Auckland's time) or Robbie Deans (when Canterbury were holders) would kick the penalty. The opposition would be dumbstruck. You'd kick off, and before you know it, they'd do it again, and you're down 10-0.

Against Counties that was virtually what we did. We thought their back three would be a bit suspect, so we put the ball behind them and caught them in possession. I caught a guy once, who didn't let the ball go, and we got three points. Then they were offside, and Mehrts dropped a goal. In about 10 minutes we were up 9-0. Inside 20 minutes Mehrts had scored a try, and we were ahead 20-6 at halftime. I began to think, "Jeez, these guys really know what it's about." In the end everything that Mehrts touched turned to gold, and although Counties got back to 23-16 soon after halftime, they were never really going to take the game. We won 42-16.

The guys were on a high after the Counties game, but we really came back to earth when we went to Athletic Park the following week, and lost to Wellington. We'd been very flat when we played Taranaki a week after winning the shield, but we scraped out a win. This time Wellington beat us 37-28. We'd had personal tragedy strike the team, with the sudden death of Richard Loe's father and Rob Penney's wife losing a baby. Sitting at home with a bad bout of the 'flu, I was amazed we even had a chance, although a slim one, of winning the game late in the second half.

We learned a very powerful lesson in Wellington. When we're fizzing and focused, we're a good side. When we're not on song we're just an average side. That's the difference between the current Canterbury side, and the Canterbury team of the Wyllie era, or the Auckland side of the late 80s and early 90s. Those teams had the personnel to win even when they weren't playing that well.

Because we lost to Wellington, the shield challenge from Otago suddenly became the one game that the success of the whole season depended on.

Let's recap what our goals were for the 1994 season…to win the shield and then hold it, to make the top four in the NPC, to have an undefeated provincial season at home. Otago had the opportunity to rob us of all those goals in the space of 80 minutes.

In Canterbury there was shield-mania again. Huge queues saw the game sold out in less than a day. Otago were unhappy about their allocation of tickets, but the toll lines burnt up between Dunedin and Christchurch as desperate Otago fans called on relatives and friends in Canterbury to hunt them down a ticket.

We had a long Tuesday training, which was a little bit flat, and on Thursday, which was another long run, we still weren't pinging the way we had been before the Waikato challenge.

But I was still reasonably happy. The pressure was probably greater on Otago than it was on us. This time Otago would head north for a challenge that most people expected them to win. I knew that in Canterbury we were ready physically, it was just a matter of getting the guys ready emotionally.

On Friday night we had the traditional captain's meeting, and I got five of the older players in the team to speak. For the first time in the week there was some real electricity in the air.

Then on Saturday morning, Vance topped it off with his prematch speech. He talked about his father and when we left the room I wasn't the only one choking back a tear. After wavering a little during the week we'd started to come together again on the Friday, and after Vance's talk we were rock solid.

I knew that we could beat Otago if we could just keep our discipline, and concentrate on our defensive screen. The Otago pattern on attack involves them not being afraid to move the ball back.

Let's take an example. Jamie Joseph takes the ball up the right hand side of the field. He's stopped, but is able to clear the ball to Stu Forster, who fires a long pass back, and to the left, to Stephen Bachop. At that stage many teams will sweep back around to cover Bachop and the players outside him. But Otago move the ball back to the right, and push the attack through there. When they moved the ball up one side, we pushed up, and kept pushing up when they swung it to the other side. When it came back, as it usually did, we knocked them over.

After winning the toss I decided to play into the wind in the first half. In the end I think our effort in the first half won us the game. While Otago scored first, with a Jamie Joseph try, and led 15-10 at halftime, Paula Bale scored two very good tries to keep us in touch. A lot of sides would have just tried to contain into the wind, but we took Otago on at their own game, stringing together four, five, even six phases.

The only time I thought we might lose the game was after Stu Forster scored five minutes after halftime. At 20-10 we were rocky if Otago scored again, and they broke up the left touch almost immediately. If they'd got more points then it would have been gone, but we regrouped, banged it back down their end, and their chance was gone.

With the wind, we had to win some ball, to give Mehrts the chance to belt it down into the corners. Then they could only try to run it out, and if we kept our screens we could knock them over, or kick for touch, and we'd get the ball for the lineout. We needed to win ball, and in the end I'd say the packs ended up 50-50. I thought we'd be able to dominate the scrums, but they'd done a lot of work there, and nobody really took control.

Before the game it had been suggested that Andrew Mehrtens was the key to Otago winning the shield. The theory was that he wouldn't have another good game with the pressure Otago would put on him. Well, he did have another good game, although this time he wasn't as dominant, because the team as a whole came together.

Play hard, train hard and enjoy it all - the All Blacks' tour of the UK, 1989.

Russell Cheyne, Allsport

**My captain Buck Shelford feeds up the ball, and I'm about to score a try for
the All Blacks against Swansea in 1989.**   Peter Bush

Jeremy Guscott lies ahead, Andy Earl is at my shoulder in support in the last game of the 1989 tour of Britain, against the Barbarians.

Peter Bush

I was a Pukekohe boy, but when the chance came to score a try against Counties, it had to be taken.

Rugby News

All Black loose forwards on the boil - A.J. Whetton and and I make the tackle on Bill Campbell, with Zinzan Brooke on hand to secure the loose ball during the second test against the Wallabies at Eden Park in 1990. The cracks were starting to show in the team. We won this test 27-17 but lost the next 21-9.

New Zealand Herald

David Campese appears to be defying gravity at Eden Park in 1990. I'm doing my best to bring him back to earth.

Brewer family collection

Test rugby is all about maintaining your concentration levels for 80 minutes. I'm obviously well focused during the 1990 second test against Australia at Eden Park.
Brewer family collection

A bevy of All Blacks, family and friends gathered for the "happy day" at Larnach's Castle, Dunedin in early 1993. Brewer family collection

Fathers and sons. Dick Brewer and Sandy Brooke line up for the camera with Zinzan and me.
Brewer family collection

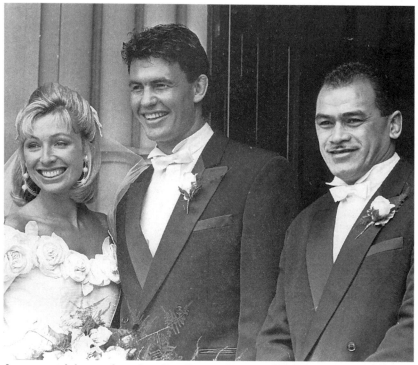

A very special occasion when Bev Keegan became Mrs Brewer. The best man, and most people's best centre too, was Joe Stanley.
Brewer family collection

Bev and me with baby Harrison. Brewer family collection

The forwards created second phase chances, and won ruck ball, while the backs did their job on attack and defence. It was very much like a test match. In fact the 1988 Otago challenge at Eden Park and the Otago challenge in '94 were as close to test match intensity and atmosphere as you would ever get. Certainly the Counties and Waikato games weren't in the same category.

With ten minutes to go, we were just one point behind. It might sound hard to believe, but I wasn't too stressed. While the stakes might not have been as high, there were many times when I'd been in a similar situation over the years. You look at the clock, and ask the referee how much time he makes it left. You think, "Right, we're getting an edge in the forwards, now we need to get down near their line, get a roll on, and they'll either infringe or miss a tackle. Then we're in."

Against Otago, with just the three points needed to keep the shield, at the back of my mind was something we'd actually practised at training. We worked at taking a penalty near halfway, kicking the ball to touch for our throw in, winning the lineout, then setting up a ruck in midfield, and Mehrts kicking a dropped goal.

Referees are not inclined to give penalties at the crucial, last gasp stage of the game, so the dropped goal is a real option with someone like Mehrts at first-five. With Stephen Bachop at first-five I'd probably have thought about scoring a try, but Mehrts will probably get four out of five dropped goals. With five minutes to go, we did it against Otago, but this was a one in five for Mehrts. He made a good dropped goal attempt, but missed.

Down to the last couple of minutes we had a lineout just metres from the Otago line. I looked at Mehrts. I didn't have to speak, he's an intelligent guy. He knew exactly what I was thinking about. We won the lineout, then were awarded the scrum. From the scrum we moved it towards the midfield. Mehrts was right behind the ruck, ready for the dropkick. But David Latta came through, and we got the penalty.

I actually got more satisfaction out of the Otago defence than when we won the shield from Waikato. It was my old home side, and I'd got two good hidings from them on the 'Brook.

Even more than that was the fact I knew the Otago players very well, and I knew just how much football means to them, how much commitment they make and how hard they train. I knew how gut wrenching it was going to be for them if they lost.

But I was happy it was my team that had won.

*　　　*　　　*

Laurie Mains: I don't have any doubt at all that if Mike Brewer had been captaining Otago they would have won the shield.

Otago had the game won and Canterbury on the rack with a quarter of an hour to go. They exhibited some looseness in their game, that had been there all year, and they gave away the ball when they were playing into the wind.

It's significant that Canterbury didn't give away any kickable penalties to Otago in the second half. That wasn't so much Canterbury's discipline, but Otago's ability to give the ball back to Canterbury whenever in an attacking situation by giving 50/50 passes, or kicking the ball to Canterbury in Canterbury's territory.

If Mike had been playing for Otago in the second half the ball wouldn't have got to the positions where it could be given away. He's very strong on ball maintenance and discipline into the wind. That's what Otago lacked.

Canterbury, on the other hand, wouldn't have played that patient waiting game without him there. Mike knew the deficiencies of Otago, and that they were likely to crack. And they did.

10

A Man to Rely On

Today I would count Richard Loe as a good friend, someone I could always rely on. But in 1990 in France I nearly broke my knuckle punching him on the head. It might not have been so unusual if it had been in a game, but it happened while we were travelling together on the All Black bus.

We'd had a couple of run-ins from the days when we were first All Black team-mates. In Australia in '88 there were some fisticuffs on the bus and it boiled over a bit two years later in France.

There was a fairly fierce argument when the team was announced for the second game of the tour. Richard was in the front row, and I had been appointed captain.

Richard made a remark to me about whether I'd been sucking up to the coach, who as it happened was Richard's uncle, Grizz Wyllie. By now I knew that Richard was one of those people with a big, gruff exterior, who was always baiting people, usually just for amusement.

This time was a little different. It seemed he had thought he should be given the chance to captain the team. I said, "Richard, if you've got any problem, come and see me." We were standing in a corridor, having a pretty frank talk, when Joe Stanley came along.

"What's going on here?" asked Joe.

"Nothing really," I replied. "Loey's got a problem about me being captain."

Joe said to Richard, "What's your problem with that?"

Richard basically told Joe to get stuffed. Now Joe was angry. For a while there was the chance they might both go outside and come to blows.

Luckily that died down, but a while later, on the bus, Richard and I started what began as a playful scuffle, in one of those attempted back seat takeovers that happen every so often on tour. For a while it got full on. I don't think Richard got hurt too much, but I bruised my knuckle and had a pretty sore jaw.

It wasn't that we were at each other's throats all the time. Players just get frustrated as you go through the tour, and next thing there's a bit of a go on the bus.

*　　*　　*

Richard Loe: Mike and I are very much the same in some regards. You want to get to the top, and you don't want people standing in the way. We've come to understand each other now, and to be friends.

The bus? It was halfway through an attempted takeover of the back seat. In those days, if you could inflict a bit of wounding, you did.

*　　*　　*

The thing I found with Richard, before we played together for Canterbury, was that he doesn't mind confronting situations. I'm a bit like that myself.

Richard is quite happy to stand up and talk things out, then he'll make his decision on what's been discussed, and get on with life. He doesn't hold things and brood over them.

As a player I certainly respected him for his ability and his strength. He's very, very strong. When Otago played Waikato we had to try to work out how to counter Richard. He was more of a problem than Graham Purvis or Warren Gatland, their other front rowers. But when you put the three of them together, they were quite lethal.

*　　*　　*

Richard Loe: If we (Waikato) played against Otago, we knew

that if we could take Bruiser out of the game we'd bugger up their game plan and their direction. I got up him and he got up me a bit. But he was the kingpin for Otago. If he was out you'd broken the camel's back.

I remember him once saying to me after Otago had played Waikato that all he and Ginge (Paul Henderson) had done all day was tackle me or Purvy (Graham Purvis) or Buck Anderson. They never saw a back or a loose forward all day. We hammered Otago a few times in Hamilton, and down there, in Dunedin, they came out on top a few times.

*　　*　　*

When Vance Stewart wanted me to captain the Canterbury side, I said we really needed someone to beef up the tight five. Not long afterwards Richard started talking with Grizz about moving to South Africa and playing for the team Grizz was coaching, Eastern Province.

Laurie Mains phoned me, and said, "Do you want Richard for the Canterbury side?"

I said, "Yeah, we'd love him. Let's see if we can get him to Christchurch."

My thinking was that for Canterbury to even have a chance of being successful in '94 we needed someone in the front row who had some physical and psychological presence about him. Someone who could really bind that tight five together, and give them some inner strength. Richard was the perfect guy for the job.

The Canterbury Rugby Union, and the sponsors, got enthused, and Richard was able to get on to a farm north of Christchurch.

There were concerns about Richard's past record. He'd been serving a ban for gouging, and there had been incidents in Australia with the All Blacks too.

Vance and I sat down, and we talked through what we expected of Richard. When Richard came down he had a meeting with Vance, and Vance outlined what we wanted.

So Richard knew the rules we played by in Canterbury, and he accepts them, and he's played by them. His behaviour has

149

been brilliant, on and off the field. What he's passed on to a young Canterbury side, the knowledge and experience, they'd be lucky to get in a lifetime.

In the All Blacks we let bygones be bygones, but Richard and I were never close the way I was with Joe Stanley, John Kirwan or AJ Whetton. One of the things I've come to really like about him in Canterbury, that's led to a much closer friendship, is the way he commits himself to the cause of Canterbury rugby, and winning for the team.

When I first came into the Canterbury team, I was tough on players if they didn't concentrate at training, didn't get there on time, didn't give it everything during a game.

Some of them must have been thinking, "This guy wants to run the show, who does he think he is?" When Richard came in, his attitude was exactly the same. That reinforced anything I wanted to say.

We began to create the tight environment that leads to success. Richard was a major part of that. I would honestly say that if we hadn't had Richard in '94 we wouldn't have won the Ranfurly Shield, and we wouldn't have made the top four in the national championship.

*   *   *

Vance Stewart: When Richard talks he generates confidence, and that was one of his roles that was important to me, his ability to act as a leader. He was very successful at getting the best response from the players. I couldn't have asked for anything more.

*   *   *

Richard Loe: I'd like to think I've been a help to Mike with his captaincy. If he says something, I back him up 100 per cent. When Mike lays down the law, and then the young ones turn round and see a silly old bugger like me doing it, they start to believe it must be the right thing. When just one person is saying this is the right way it can be rejected.

One person couldn't have changed things around in Canterbury. But we had Mike, who's a great thinker of the game, he gives the direction, then there's someone like myself who can put it into action in the forwards, Graeme Bachop, who was a great influence, and you've got Mike's ability to give the young backs plenty of confidence.

When I arrived, not everyone was getting on too well, but that's all been pushed out the back door. A couple have left, a few new chaps have come in, and everyone really knows where we're going. We've all pulled together.

Vance has been interesting. He doesn't mind leaving it to Mike or myself to pull them into line if they need it. We'd work as a team. At times Mike would decide he needed to change a bootlace, just to leave me with the team at training. They'd get a bigger snarling from me than they would from Mike.

*   *   *

Richard demands a lot at training. He's very similar to me in that respect. He doesn't stand for mistakes either. Having Richard reinforcing me at training was a big plus.

As for Richard's behaviour during a game, that's been exemplary. I was appalled when he was cited after the Otago game, for allegedly stomping John Timu. That was an absolute nonsense.

Basically what it comes down to with Richard is man management. It's true he plays the game right to the letter of the law, which comes from his ingrained determination that his side must win the game.

There is pressure from the public, the media, even from friends and family, on sports people to win. It's not just in rugby, but in soccer, cricket, athletics, any major sport. If you don't win, people can be very ruthless. Just ask the New Zealand cricket team. I believe that pressure would have contributed to times in the past where Richard has overstepped the mark.

Also, in the years before the Greg Cooper incident, I don't believe that Richard was well served by the New Zealand Rugby Union and the All Blacks management.

Like most of the Otago team I wasn't as outraged or shocked by what happened to Greg in the 1992 provincial final as many people in New Zealand seemed to be. I'd been through the experience of playing in France in 1986, when after every game I played I needed stitches in my head. In every game players tried to gouge my eyes. In every game I had my testicles grabbed and twisted.

That sort of behaviour is not accepted in rugby now, but nobody ever told Richard that when Carozza got an elbow in the face in Brisbane in '92 that it was unacceptable. If Richard had been pulled aside then, slapped on the wrist, even given a limited suspension, there would never have been the outcry after what happened with Greg.

From my perspective, captaining Otago that day in Hamilton, it was a spur of the moment reaction from Richard, a bit like a loose forward in the old days being tempted to late tackle a good first five. You might have got penalised in the past, but he might have to leave the field.

Sure, Richard overstepped the mark, but I really don't believe it would have been blown up the way it was if people hadn't believed he'd got away with things in the past. If it had been an isolated incident there wouldn't have been the outcry.

Here's a guy who plays to the limits. He gets away with things, he gets away with things, then, bang, TV gets him, and it's not just a brick falling on him, the whole wall comes down.

Poor management at national level was then followed by an over-reaction in the committee room. There have been some shocking stomping incidents where players were not punished anywhere as severely as Richard was.

When he came to Canterbury it was soon obvious that he was under intense pressure, unable to step out of line 10 per cent of what any other player in the country could do.

In one of our early games in '94 a first division referee apologised for having a very bad match. He said, "I know I had a shocker. From the time I went on the field I just watched Richard." That's a first division referee!

Obviously some other teams have tried to provoke him. People have tried to poke him in the eyes, stick fingers up his nose, but he's been very, very good.

*   *   *

Vance Stewart: When Richard came to Canterbury we had a

talk, and agreed on standards that were acceptable. I take my hat off to him. He adhered to those standards right throughout the season. At no stage did he step out of line.

At stages he was provoked, but he controlled his feelings. He tried so hard to do the right thing, and I felt he succeeded. That's why it was so disappointing when he was cited after the Otago game.

*   *   *

I think Richard has done marvelously well to come back to the top level after being suspended for so long after the Greg Cooper affair. He and his family were under enormous pressure, but he came back. That's probably a reflection of the determination and grit of the guy.

When the Canterbury Rugby Union were talking to me about David Campese possibly playing at the end of '95, we were talking about the market value of players.

I was very upfront about it. If we were going to put market value on the success of the team, I would place Richard Loe ahead of David Campese. Campo might put bums on seats, but if it came to replacing Campo or replacing Loey, it'd be much harder to replace Richard. He's had such a lot to do with Canterbury's success.

*   *   *

Richard Loe: It's a more united feeling in the Canterbury team than I ever had in Waikato. Canterbury are a team waiting to happen. They're probably not anywhere at their peak yet.

I know with the tight five, I have to keep my standards up, but if any one of them is not prepared to work the way I do, they can get jumped on. The loosies know that Mike can play all three positions, so they need to keep up to scratch, or he could take their place.

Mike is a very conscientious captain. He'll watch a video over and over after a game, and come to training with four foolscap pages of notes. He really thinks things through, looking at what the backs are doing right, what they're doing wrong.

If I watch a video, I tend to look to make sure that I'm doing the basics, and if I'm not, who's preventing me from doing them.

I want to see that my back garden's okay before I look at anyone else's.

The backs know that Mike's watching them, and if they do it wrong they'll be growled at. I'll do it too. I say to backs, "I may not be able to do it myself, but I've played with fellows who can do it very, very well." Once you know what's meant to be done, there are really no excuses.

*   *   *

Richard and I have talked about, and had a laugh over, the times our differences of opinion got physical. Now we can get on.

He's a very interesting character. He's a real man's man, with a few rough edges. But if you ever had to rely on someone in a tight situation, I'd rather rely on Richard than many, many other people.

11

Simply the Best

The best rugby player I've ever seen, or played with or against, is now pulling on the jersey of the Auckland Warriors league team.

John Kirwan could step you, step and fend you, or just run around you. At his best, when he wanted to beat his man on a football field it wasn't a case of if he would, it was a case of when and how.

In my time there has never been another player anywhere in the world who could do that at will. Playing against him when he was in the Auckland rugby jersey you had to have two or three men to cover him. One on one there was nobody in the game able to hold him. He was quick, he could step, and he was strong. If a guy managed to get hold of him, JK could fend him off.

When he came to Dunedin, playing for Auckland, he got a bit of stick from the crowd, because as far as the Carisbrook crowd was concerned it was definitely here come the flowerpots from the big city when Auckland ran on the 'Brook.

But they still respected him as a player. I think the Otago crowd are as good as any in the world for recognising quality in a player, and though Otago were always fired up for the Auckland game, the Carisbrook crowd got to see flashes of his best. In fact there would be very few spectators round New Zealand, or round the world, who wouldn't carry a memory or two of JK when he was running hot, and that was a brilliant sight.

Obviously John Kirwan would fill most of the requirements you would need if you were putting together a dream team.

My thoughts on positional play, and the players who meet those requirements, would begin with the front row, the concrete mixers, the first point of confrontation.

They need as a trio to have a physical presence that borders on being intimidating, and to form a dominating platform in scrums, where they can gain a psychological advantage over their opponents.

In lineouts the props need to be blocks and support the jumpers, while the hooker puts the ball right on the mark when he throws in. All three need to hit rucks and mauls with pace and power. If they want to run with the ball like the flowery loose forwards, that's fine, but get the basics right first.

Locks are much the same. As the biggest men in the team they can create huge damage if they hunt together, and hit rucks and mauls together. In the lineout they need more than one type of jump, so they don't get too predictable to the opposition. Locks must be very good scrummagers, with flexibility, strength, and good body position.

Like the props, running with the ball can only be a bonus for locks. They need to have those skills, like a Robin Brooke, but like Robin, they need to know what job comes first.

Loose forwards MUST work as a team. They're usually the decision makers when there's a breakdown, and it's imperative that each man makes the right decision as they arrive one after the other.

The first makes the decision whether to pick up or drive, the second makes the decision whether to drive or run off, and so does the third. They're crucial as to how a ruck or maul is set up.

First and foremost, the loose forward is part of a pack of eight who want to win quality ball going forwards. If you can't do that, there is very little point in giving the ball to your backs. Unless they're getting front foot ball, all a back can really do is to kick.

The next role is to get out faster to the breakdown than the opposition. But then comes the difference between the good and the also-ran loosies. Some can get to the breakdown, but don't have the fitness, the strength, or possibly the skill, to turn that breakdown into continuity of attack. The aim should be to keep the game going, rather than setting up a ruck. That's where being able to complement each other as a trio becomes important.

The first role is to support the tight five to get the dominance, and then freeing yourself up to guarantee continuity.

Ideally all the backs should be able to beat a man one on one, whether by stepping a man with the ball in hand, or freeing up a team-mate with a pass.

Defensively a back must be strong enough to contain his own man, and also develop other aspects, of passing, kicking and punting until they're second nature.

So to have a very, very good backline you need brilliance and togetherness. The brilliance to make individual breaches of the opposing line, the togetherness to know each other's play so well you run off each other, and defensively have the confidence to know that everyone in the backline will play his part in the defensive screen.

Among All Black backs I played with Joe Stanley (Bullet) would read a game better than anyone I've known. I'd say he would read it even better than Grant Fox.

It took very little time after first getting to know Bullet in the Baby Blacks to respect him as a player who thought a lot about his own backline, and what they were trying to achieve, and then what the opposition were trying to do.

He had an intensely analytical mind, and he was very fast at summing up what the opposition were up to.

The classic example came in 1994, at Mt Smart Stadium, in John Kirwan's farewell rugby game. The Australian Barbarians were pulling a move, and Joe read it as though he'd called it himself. He nailed their fullback.

My philosophy that a back must be able to beat a man, either one on one, or with a pass, is satisfied in Joe's case by his passing, which I believe was unquestionably the best of any back in union or league in his era.

He could put the ball perfectly outside the man marking his wing, inside the man marking his wing, or, if the fullback came in, have it sitting up and waiting for him.

Backplay is all about having a distributor or a penetrator, and in most cases Joe was the distributor.

People talk about JK, or John Gallagher, or Terry Wright, but the secret weapon behind all of them was Joe. He put the ball where they wanted it when they were at pace. It would have been so much harder for them if it had been half a metre behind them, and they'd had to check their run to make sure they took the pass.

But they knew, as penetrators, that when they were going through a move the ball would be in the right spot. That was Joe's great ability, putting the ball to within an inch of where the penetrator wanted it.

We haven't had a centre with Joe's passing skills since he left the All Blacks, and let's remember that when Joe Stanley retired, that was the last of the best we saw of John Kirwan.

I think Joe's loss to the All Blacks was much greater than many would perceive. Not just for his on field brilliance, but also for his qualities off it. He was a real father figure. Players had just so much respect for him, because he knew what he was talking about.

And basically he was the only one who could control Foxy. What Joe said, Foxy basically did, and that's difficult, because Foxy's got a very strong personality.

Not that I thought Foxy was too demanding. Some players might have, but I'm very demanding myself. With Foxy everything had to be precise, and right on the button.

On the field he was very intense, and he wanted everything structured. It worked very well for Auckland, the most successful provincial side ever in New Zealand, where players knew, from set piece to second phase to third phase, where the ball was going to be.

They were such talented players in that Auckland side, and when they knew where the ball was going they got there quickly, and had the brilliance to absolutely take another team to bits.

However, for a team to keep winning they have to keep progressing, and really, between '87 and '91, at All Black level we didn't further develop and evolve our style of play, which revolved around Foxy calling structured moves. So we became a little bit predictable, and the opposition watched what we were doing, and began to counter it. Within Foxy's own make up and nature, we couldn't kick out of that.

He was the perfect tradesman though, and he put an enormous amount of work in to maintain that. He was like a golfer or a tennis player. If a swing or a serve doesn't work, they go to a coach until it's corrected. Foxy would keep things very simple, and make sure everything was exactly as it should be.

His attitude at training was reflected in the best All Black teams of his era. Foxy trained with precision, and so did we. We trained to not make mistakes.

I'm not just talking about the obvious things, like not dropping the ball, but players running perfect lines, body positions being perfect, being in the right place to accept a pass if someone needed to pass it to you. Foxy demanded that everyone else have as much precision in their game as he did.

Foxy was in a pivotal position, so he called most of the shots in the All Blacks. If Buck Shelford wasn't happy with the call he'd overcall him, but that would happen only two or three times in a game.

Buck Shelford would be the most inspirational footballer I've ever played with. He was very much a "follow me boys" leader, and if you were good enough to stay within a metre of him he'd take you through the front lines.

If you looked at how Buck approached rugby, he wouldn't be the scholar that David Kirk was, or even a young Andrew Mehrtens, but he put a lot of time into his rugby, and he was a lot more analytical than people give him credit for. He summed up a game very well.

Buck was fortunate, as we all were, to have someone as analytical as Foxy at first-five. If there were four options available, you could almost guarantee that Foxy would choose the right one, the one with the highest percentage chance of success.

Buck didn't often overcall Foxy, and if Buck did it was usually because he wanted the forwards to gain just a little bit more dominance to totally control the game. That was one of the things we were so often able to do during Buck's time as captain.

At training Buck wasn't a great talker, and didn't get too wound up. But when it came to the match, that's when he showed his true colours. He led from the front, and only got emotive if other players were not giving it 120 per cent the way he always did.

When you have a leader who is so physically committed, he'll constantly lift you during a game. Rugby does demand that you put your body on the line, and Buck answered that challenge more readily than any player I've known.

Zinzan Brooke is a player who really has as much talent and skill as Michael Jones, but it took Zinny until 1990 to show his true qualities as an All Black, and I don't think it was until 1992, with Laurie Mains as coach, that Zinny really became the complete footballer he is now.

In 1988 and '89 Zinny struggled in the All Blacks, and even in '91, when he was carrying an injury, he struggled again.

But I think the problems he had coming to grips with international play went beyond injuries. Playing for Auckland when they were so dominant in New Zealand wasn't the best thing for Zinny's development as an individual player.

His role in the Auckland side in the late 80s was very much as a support player. Their tight five was so commanding the Auckland loosies didn't have to push too hard in the scrums, they didn't have to work too hard on defence, and they got all the ball they wanted. They just got out around the backs, and acted as link players.

It would have been fantastic to be in a side like that, but when it came to playing in other teams, that found themselves more evenly matched, there were other roles for a loose forward to play.

There were other lines to run. You have to go up a lot shallower, a lot flatter, in your defensive screen in a tight match, you can't just run your purely attacking lines.

Going backwards is a lot different, and I think Zinny took a while to come to terms with the complete role of a forward going back as well as forwards.

Fitzy had to persuade Laurie to give Zinny a chance in the All Blacks in '92, but, after that shaky start, I honestly think it was Laurie who really helped Zinny to understand that part of being a good No 8 is to go backwards as well as forwards.

Zinny lacked certain qualities when he was playing for Auckland, but from '92 onwards he now fully understands the roles he has to play on attack and defence, and he's realised the enormous potential that was always there.

When you look at raw talent Michael Jones, the Iceman, is right up there with JK. I first saw Michael in action at the Colts trial in '85, and then on the Barbarians tour in ' 87. Right from the time Ice scored two tries in the Colts trial (and still, somehow, missed out on the team) it was obvious he was something special.

Over the years I've come to the conclusion that what makes Michael so very special is that he's the most intuitive player I've ever seen. People who saw Waka Nathan at his best say that was Waka's biggest attribute too.

A great player like John Kirwan knows what he's going to do when he gets the ball, and he knows what move is on. But Michael goes a step further. As a fullback goes up to take a high ball, Ice will judge the flight of the ball, see the angle of the fullback, and will move his line, just in case it bounces off a certain way.

People talk about people being in the right place at the right time. In rugby I think that's the result of intuition. Michael always seems to know how a game will evolve, and if a backline move is going to break down, where it will be. If there's a breakdown he'll be there, and he has such huge skills, he can turn defence into attack.

And he does have remarkable skills. Graeme Bachop and I still talk about the '88 tour to Australia with the All Blacks, when the level of intensity of training was so high, that we used to be scared to go to training.

You feared to go, in case you made a mistake. As one of the younger players at the time it took a lot of the fun out of the game, but from the point of view of the team, it was very good for results.

Whether it was touch football, or a drill, everything was intensely competitive. If you made a mistake at touch, your own team just roasted you, and so did the guys you were playing against. That's just how it was.

Zinny was one of the kings of competition. Everything was for the world championship, whether it was touch, 10 pin bowling, to tossing coins closest to a line at an airport. The competitiveness went from there, to training, on to the field in a game.

We went out on the paddock competing with ourselves to not make mistakes, and to have a fair war with the guy in our position to try to play your way into the test team. That sort of competition, where everybody is working hard and playing well, is actually healthy. When everyone is performing, you have an harmonious side.

But despite the best efforts of everyone on tour, we were men, not machines, and at every training there would be two or three mistakes. After three weeks all of us had made at least one mistake at training - except Michael.

It got uncanny. Three weeks, no mistake. Four weeks, no mistake. In the fifth week he actually dropped a pass at training. Everyone just stopped dead and looked at him. Somebody said, "Are you okay?" The immediate conclusion being sprung to was that he must be sick, and need a break. He wasn't. He'd just shown that he was actually human.

Physically, Michael has everything a loose forward needs. He's got a very strong upper body, and he's a beautiful lateral mover. He would be as physically talented as anyone I've ever seen, even Zinny, who, like Michael, is strong, can run, and is a good tackler. But Michael's a fantastic jumper in the lineout as well, and that's one purely physical attribute he has over Zinny.

The most gifted athlete among the really big men I've seen in rugby would be Gary Whetton.

Gary is agile, well balanced, very fast and very strong. His agility made him a good jumper in the lineout, and when it came to scrums he provided real strength. The Auckland scrum of the late 1980s and early 1990s wasn't so good just because of the front row. Gary's strength and technique in behind them at lock was a major factor too.

He actually had it all, because when the time came to handle the ball he had exceptional skills. In fact, I'd say he was the first real athlete we had at lock since Colin Meads. People sometimes forget that Pinetree wasn't just tough, he had the whole range of rugby skills.

AJ Whetton didn't have the natural gifts of his twin brother Gary, but AJ had a passion to succeed, and he loathed failing, for both himself and the team.

He's probably the man who, in 1987, turned blindside flanker into a specialist position in this country. Over the years we had sometimes played two openside flankers in test matches, but after the World Cup in '87 we've accepted that they're specialist positions.

AJ turned a mistake in the '86 test in Dunedin against the Wallabies, when he missed the tackle on Steve Tuynman for the famous "try that wasn't", and his disappointment at being dropped for the tour to France at the end of that year, into powerful spurs for him to perform in the first World Cup.

He was extremely fit at the start of '87, and in the Cup his precision, his lines, his support play were just superb. Add in the fact that he became the best jumper in the world at the back of the lineout, and for my money he was the player of the tournament in '87, even against challengers like John Kirwan and Michael Jones.

As Foxy was the complete tradesman at first-five, so AJ became the complete tradesman as a blindside flanker.

For a front row that, as a unit, will dominate the first point of confrontation for you, it's hard for me to go past Steve McDowell, Sean Fitzpatrick and Richard Loe. Together, at their best, which was before the fitness problems of the '91 World Cup, they were intimidating, and they complemented each other.

Steve and Sean were so good with the ball in hand, while Richard was so strong in scrums and rucks and mauls. He was the anchor.

One who never got the accolades he probably deserved as a tighthead prop was John Drake. If you looked at him off the field, or even on it, he didn't look hard enough to hold up a scrum, but in fact he was a real exponent of the position. One of the strengths of that World Cup side in '87 was the scrummaging, and that was an area that John focused on, and took real pride in.

In the Otago side a lot of our game revolved around our loose forward trio, and at what I think was our best we had Brent Pope at No 8, Ginge Henderson on the openside, and myself at blindside.

Popey was an amazing impact player. He had a rare ability to break the game open with one big run. He was very strong in the upper body and when he ran from the base of the scrum he could rip a defence to shreds. Then, when he was clear of the traffic in the open field he could keep going, because he had genuine speed. He would certainly have made an excellent league player.

Probably the only thing that went against him in rugby, possibly to the point of holding him back from an international career, was that he could never get too enthused about training.

He left everything on the track in a game, but I guess a lot of coaches like to see a player giving it 100 per cent in training as well as when he's playing. But that's how Popey was. He would never pretend he was wild about the training runs.

Of course, he was also unlucky that he was in the All Black area of Buck Shelford and Zinzan Brooke. I believe that if he had got into the All Blacks he would have been a very good All Black. A lot of international players wouldn't have known his style of play, and he would have made some huge runs in an All Black jersey.

While there were many classy backs in the country in the late 1980s, Otago did not have a player who could cut open a backline until John Timu came along.

I saw JT stand up a man, and then go outside him without a hand being laid on him, in his first games for Otago, and he really got better and better as time went on.

My disappointment for JT is that he had to challenge John

Kirwan for the right wing spot in the All Blacks, and, to my mind, JT mastered the position. But he was a right wing, and that's it. It was a shame he was ever shifted to fullback.

I don't believe that JT ever got on top of the attacking side of playing fullback. Defensively he was very good, because he was fast, very strong, and he was an excellent tackler.

But the hangover we've had at national level since John Gallagher went is that we've wanted to find this fullback who can come in anywhere in the backline, from outside the second-five, to outside the winger, and carve up the opposition with pace and timing.

By the time JT was at fullback the forwards weren't dominating the way they were when Kipper was at fullback, so JT always had the opposing loosies hanging out, helping to push the defensive screen across to him. He was never given the space that Kipper was. So it was a tougher time to be a fullback running into the All Black backline, and somehow JT was never able to master the lines and timing the way he had on the right wing.

He's made an immediate impression in league, and I'm sure he'll be a very good player in the game. They won't fault his tackling, and with a bit of space to run in, knowing he doesn't have to let the ball go, he'll beat a man when the opposition kicks.

JT is also very strong. He'd be one of the strongest backs in the world on his feet, which he showed for Otago every time we played Auckland, and he marked Inga Tuigamala.

The first time they played against each other in a Ranfurly Shield challenge, in 1988, Inga bumped off JT's first attempt at a tackle. JT just gritted his teeth, came in for a second go, and crashed Inga to the ground. From then on he covered Inga all day and made the afternoon a nightmare for him. As time went by JT outplayed Inga whenever he marked him, continually driving him back in tackles.

Paul Henderson is a player who has so often been in a similar position to the one Popey found himself in with Buck and Zinny. If not for Michael Jones I believe Paul would have had a very long, distinguished career for the All Blacks.

Ginge is one of those hard, self-made players from the deep

south. He didn't have a host of other good players around him to push him on, but went out and trained hard himself. He made the shift to Otago to make the All Blacks, and in a stronger team he was very quickly in the black jersey.

Ginge was fantastic at getting to the loose ball first, and if it was on the ground he was never scared to throw his body down to win it. In the long run it has cost him at times, because that's when you get injuries, never being afraid to risk your body the way he does.

He's an extremely good runner with the ball, and one of the best tacklers in the game. He was a delight to work with in a loose forward trio, because you knew within your loose forward pattern you didn't have to worry about what Ginge was going to do. He virtually never made a mistake.

The one game that sticks out more in my memory than any other with Ginge is the '88 shield challenge. Between Ginge, the inside backs and myself we virtually closed the Auckland backs down. I remember Joe Stanley coming back on the cut a couple of times early on, and we hammered him. I would say on that day we were the match of the Auckland trio, Zinny, AJ and Michael Jones.

Timing can make such a difference for a player in a specialist position, and if Ginge had been in a different era to Michael Jones, I believe he would have played a lot of test matches.

In the Canterbury team there are several players with a heap of raw talent, but if you look to one who has already performed with that talent, the standout must be Andrew Mehrtens.

Mehrts can run, he can punt, he can drop kick and place kick, he's a good passer, he can step, and, with a bit of guidance and nurturing, he just needs to refine those skills until they're perfect.

I think Andrew can become a footballer who's something of a mixture of Grant Fox and Frano Botica, and be as good, in his way, as either. He might not have the precision and intensity of Foxy, but he's starting to understand the pressures and rigours of top football.

One of the best things about Mehrts is his fairly carefree nature, and he's a very, very intelligent young man. Through his schooling and general life, I believe he treats everything as a challenge, because of his intelligence.

But now he understands a bit more of the percentage game, although I like the fact that while he understands it, and can read what the low risk option is, he's still flamboyant.

That creates uncertainty in the opposition. If you have a very good side that comes up against a highly structured team, the structured team is almost easy to read.

Foxy was very structured in his play, so if a strong team could match Auckland or the All Blacks in the forwards, they didn't have to worry about Foxy running, or doing something sensational to cut them open.

That was really what happened in Dublin in the '91 World Cup semifinal. The forwards weren't performing, so Foxy was getting static ball, and he didn't have that touch of brilliance with the ball in hand to create doubt and uncertainty in the opposition. The Aussies just ran off him all day onto the second-five and centre, and cut the attacks off there.

In my ideal backline everyone can beat a man one on one from halfback to fullback, and a player like Mehrts and a player like Frano can do that.

Mehrts has another attacking skill that can be vital in a close game. He's a lethal dropkicker, and that can win easy points when you really need them. When you're playing against a good dropkicker it's a real thorn in your side.

Canterbury coach, Vance Stewart, has said of Mehrts that if there are two options available, Mehrts will choose the hard one, just to test himself, and I think that's actually true. However, I firmly believe he'll more and more determine which option to take to give his side an advantage, and in such a pivotal position that's essential. We're watching the emergence of a very, very good footballer.

Looking at some other stars of the future, I think all teams need a leader, a hard nut, in the tight five, and Anton Oliver would be the best I've seen in the under-19s, or Colts. Anton's father, Frank, was famous as one of the old style, unyielding hard men of the game, and for such a young bloke Anton is already a pretty intimidating player.

Anton is very strong in the lower body, and as time goes by he'll get stronger in the upper body too. He's certainly hungry and hard, and if I had a criticism of him it's that as a hooker his throwing in to the lineout needs to be more accurate.

When Dave Latta retires I can see Anton moving into the Otago front row, and quickly establishing himself as a dominant figure. I like tight forwards who have a real physical presence about them.

Taine Randall would be one of the most talented players to emerge since Michael Jones, and the only difficulty I could see would be what position Taine is best suited to.

He's quite short by the standards of international loose forwards, but, a bit like Michael, he's got a big vertical jump, and, a bit like Michael, he's intuitive, intelligent, fast, keen and with fantastic skills.

Eventually he might have to play openside flanker, because if he makes the All Blacks they'll need two tall loosies with him. When the lineouts get cramped, and you can't really jump, it makes it easier for the tall guys to win the ball.

Although he's young, Taine's a good leader, and I think he could captain the All Blacks in the future.

Tabai Matson, the Canterbury centre, is going to have to work hard at his game, but he has huge potential. He lacks a wee bit of speed, both off the mark and top end speed, and he needs to watch his weight.

But he has extremely good ball skills, and he's the type of player who can stand in the tackle and offload the ball to a player running off a short pass. As defensive screens get more sophisticated that's a great ability to possess. With the right direction and coaching he could become a good international.

Glen Osborne is possibly the answer to what everyone's been looking for since Kipper Gallagher went to league, the fast, agile, skilled fullback who can beat a man, and cut open a backline. Given the confidence and backing he could really come of age as our No 1 fullback over the next few years.

Oz is a bit like Andy Earl, bigger and stronger than he looks in a rugby jersey. He's wiry and strong, takes knocks well, and when he makes tackles he hits quite hard. In fact, defensively he's very good. He can tackle head on, and he has the speed to cover threequarters who try to beat him on the outside.

Jonah Lomu threatened to be the enigma of New Zealand rugby. With the ball in hand he's potentially as good as JK, able to beat a man any way he wants to.

But in the months before the World Cup his own laziness almost cost him a place in the All Black camp at the end of the year. He was the least aerobically fit man there.

His talk during the year about wanting to be a good All Black looked cheap. He could talk the talk, but there were signs he couldn't walk the walk.

The shock of being publically named as a player who hadn't measured up did him good, he dug in, and by the time we reached South Africa he was up to speed.

Now the question is whether he can maintain the form from the World Cup. It could be that he needs a professional environment, whether in rugby or league, to make sure he does the work that will keep him one of the sensations of football. Physically he has everything needed to be one of the game's greats.

While we're talking of league, as well as John Timu and JK, the "ones who got away" over the last five years, Frano Botica, John Gallagher, Johnny Schuster, Matt Ridge and Inga all shared something in common. They were very good attacking players, but none of them were that flash in defence.

But league is basically an attacking game, and it was their skill with the ball in hand that got them headhunted in the first place.

Most of them have improved other skills since they've gone to league, and Frano's goalkicking would be the prime example. He started doing a lot more work on his kicking when he was in Italy, but once he went to Wigan, and was being paid for it, his kicking moved to another plane.

When he was still playing rugby Frano never put real pressure on Foxy for the All Blacks' first-five spot because he wasn't anything like the goalkicker Foxy was then, or Frano is now.

If he'd been kicking like that as a rugby player Frano would have been first choice, I'm sure, because he could beat a man with a step, and he offered another superb skill, his backing up. Frano wasn't just very fast, which he was, but he was also very fit. A lot of backs say they don't like doing aerobic running, clocking up big distances, but Frano ran and ran and ran.

When he was in a game he was then able to back up tirelessly, because he had that strength and endurance. Time and again he backed up outside his wing. He certainly needed a heap of speed for that, but he also needed to be superbly fit. Frano always was.

Johnny Schu was a back who could beat a man with classy footwork, or he could chip over the top and recover. He was a beautiful passer too, and he formed a relationship with players that at times was almost uncanny.

He and John Gallagher seemed to just know what the other was going to do on the field, and Schu started to form that relationship with Joe Stanley when Schu went to league. Joe and Schu were a good match. Joe was the rock and the distributor, while Schu was the mover and the shaker, the high stepper. He was a very classy attacking player, but, again, he wasn't flash on defence.

Kipper Gallagher was much the same. A fantastic attacking player, a lot quicker than he looked when he ran because of the length of his stride, with perfect timing when he came into the backline. He was fortunate that his skills were complemented by Joe and Schu, who could put the ball exactly on the mark for him.

Kipper's weak area was defence, but when he was in the All Blacks he didn't have to make many tackles, and it's like any skill. If you don't have to make your tackles in a game, you actually lose the ability to do so.

Matthew Ridge could have been as good an All Black fullback as Kipper, if not better. Positionally he was very sound, and while he wasn't as quick as Kipper he was very quick, with a range of all round skills.

The edge that Ridgey had was an arrogance about him that made him believe he would be a success. With that attitude he could see he was going to go places, and very early he decided he'd made a good living out of it, which he has.

On the subject of Inga, I agree entirely with Fitzy who suggested that Inga, while very strong, and very difficult to contain with the ball in hand, was also a lazy rugby player.

No other player, in my experience, has ever got away with going on an All Black tour weighing 107kg, and, after two months of almost daily compulsory training on tour, ending at 95kg. In other words he was 12kg overweight at the start of the tour, and we really only got two weeks of his best football from him.

He really shouldn't have been in the side. In the early games his work rate, other than what he had to do on the wing, would be next to nothing. At the end of the tour he'd be popping up on the other wing, hunting the ball, which is what he should have been doing from the start.

Inga was notorious for being a lazy trainer. At his Ponsonby club people can recall his list of excuses for not doing any hard work. They ranged from the usual sore hamstring and sore ankle, to his most famous, the claim he had dust in his eye when the coach called for a gutbuster.

I got very disappointed, and I would imagine Michael Jones did too, when Inga said that training for league was much harder than training for rugby.

And if there's a message in this chapter, it's for the young, promising players I've mentioned. All of them have the potential to be very good international players, with a lot of hard work.

How good they become, how well they realise their potential, is now down to them. If they put in the work they'll reap the rewards.

12

Follow Me

If there's a strong character in a group, who is designated the leader, and stands up and says "follow me", I'll happily go along if I believe in the person.

On the other hand, if there are no strong characters, and I think I can take some responsibility, I'm one of those people who will volunteer, even to the extent of assuming responsibility until someone comes along and says, "Sorry, you're not the leader."

I really enjoyed Buck Shelford's captaincy because I had enormous respect for him, and because he was the ultimate "follow me" man.

Just the way he held himself, and the mana he had with his players and the public, earned my respect, and when you went on the field with him, the way he played the game made your respect just grow and grow.

Buck only said what he had to say at training. He really left most of his talking to the field, and even then, it wasn't much. He developed the loyalty and respect by leading from the front, with his body on the line.

At training his whole philosophy was pretty much old school. He believed that the forwards were there to dominate the set pieces and the rucks and mauls, which meant doing the physical work without too much of the glamour stuff.

He wanted every scrum given 100 per cent, lineouts won, or pressure put on the opposition, and when you got to rucks you had to bind, then hit the ruck with enough force to move it backwards, even if the opposition had the ball. So he put the tight forwards down to quite finite tasks, with the aim that the plums, running with the ball, would come later.

It was very much the same with the loosies. He wanted a contribution to the set piece before they even worried about where the ball was going.

Once the ball had gone loose the loose forwards were to work in unison, not just get there together. The whole emphasis was on the loose forward trio getting there like a wave, not all three racing each other to get there first. As each man arrived he would make a decision.

At international level the timing was one, pause, two, pause, three, at about the pace you read that. That's how quick a test match is. But if you have one there, and bang, he's tackled, then the next there, and bang, he's tackled, then when the third gets the ball he can usually get through and keep the movement alive.

If you look at the tight situations the All Blacks got into during Buck's captaincy, he rarely had to revert to simple processes to get the team back on track. Generally there were enough experienced and talented players in the team to instinctively know what had to be done next, before the call was even made.

Buck also got to know his players well. Every player likes to be built up differently, and while you can build up a team collectively, where you get your biggest benefits is when you talk to the players one on one.

You may need to talk aggressively to one player to get the best out of him. Another you may need to build up, tell him he's the best in the world in his position, and that when he's on top of his game nobody can touch him.

Most of all you need to know their capabilities, what they can do, and, just as importantly, what they can't do.

One of the other things, which comes from experience, is reading, and having a feel for, a game, then choosing the right options depending on how the game's developing. A captain can earn a lot of respect from his players when, in a tight game, he makes a split second call, and it works.

It's like anything. If you're following someone and he makes the right decision, and you all come out alive, you'll follow him again.

The other key aspect is that if you're the captain you need to be able to practice what you preach. If you're the captain you should be the fittest player in the team, so whatever is asked, you can be out in front saying, "Come on." If that's the case you basically have the right to make demands on the other players, without recriminations.

The way that Buck prepared himself, it was very obvious that he didn't just bowl up to training, and bowl up to the game. Some of the players might not have realised it, but I'm sure Buck was putting in a tremendous amount of mental preparation behind the scenes. His whole attitude was that he wanted to win every game he played as captain.

In fact, Buck covered all the requirements. He mixed well when he thought it was time to mix, but he kept just a little gap between himself and the players.

It's something I've tried a wee bit to include in my captaincy. To stay just far enough away to look objectively at the team. Then, when it comes to a hard decision about who should be playing, you're not so close to a player you let it cloud your judgment over who is playing the best rugby.

Buck might have relaxed even more, but I think he was always aware that there was a lobby pushing for Gary Whetton to be captain. But he was a superb leader, and as time went by he got stronger and stronger as a captain. That's why it was so disappointing when he was dropped.

By contrast with Buck's knowledge of his players, Jock Hobbs, who led the tour to France at the end of 1986, was someone I never got to know at all.

He seemed very much on his own during that tour, perhaps because of the pressures from the Cavaliers trip, and the apparent split between the Cavaliers and David Kirk. Jock never came to the back of the bus, and I never saw him to have a drink with.

You have to spend time with the guys to actually get to know them. I like to sit in the physio room, to see who the joker is, who wants to be left alone, who the serious guy is, who likes company, who wants to flick a ball around, and finds it impossible to sit still.

Then, when the big games arrive, you can see the changes in personality. You can't notice those changes if you're sitting in your hotel room.

So while Jock was in charge of the onfield decisions in France in '86, the leadership and direction was certainly driven by BJ Lochore. Everything I learned as a new player on the tour came from BJ, Cowboy Shaw and Wayne Shelford. Apart from that, there wasn't anything passed on.

David Kirk was one of the better captains. He was certainly a thinker of the game.

Kirky looked in depth at how a team can develop a pattern to suit strengths and cover weaknesses, and during training he helped a team develop its style, and individual players develop their own game too.

I first met him with the University A team in Dunedin, which he captained, and he was very good with on field calls and direction. Everything was very precise, and being in the pivotal position of halfback made things easy.

He read the game so well that on the paddock he could help you, as a young player, with your decision making, even with details as to what lines you should be running.

Where he was a little different from Buck was that when things got tough Kirky could blow a valve. He'd rant and rave when something went wrong, where Buck would just absorb the pressure, and try to get the guys back on track.

Kirky flatted with us for about six months while he finished med school, and I've always enjoyed his company and friendship over the years. In his playing days he basically got on well with all the guys, but possibly because he's such an intelligent person, some of the older, more basic guys might have felt a bit threatened by him. Sometimes they tried to put him in what they saw as his place, man to man. I always felt a bit sorry about that.

Having said that, Kirky is certainly not backward himself in picking holes with people's performances, and people's personalities.

I remember Kirky telling me I should go to Oxford University to become well read. He said, "You're not a complete person unless you're well read." I said that was garbage.

He couldn't understand that some people are happy in their lives as what they are, and what they want to be. Not everybody wants to be regarded as a scholar, and to be able to quote Socrates.

Even though Kirky's such an intelligent and successful person, I do think he carries a wee chip on his shoulder still, that he wasn't regarded as a great All Black, and that since the World Cup in '87, things have never quite come off for him to the level he worked hard for. When he won the Rhodes scholarship to Oxford and changed courses from medicine to political science, economics and philosophy, we all said he was going into politics. Although he worked on the Prime Minister's staff, he missed nomination as a Parliamentary candidate himself. He was dropped as Wellington rugby coach. It's a shame that he has developed a habit of picking faults in other people. In 1991 at John Kirwan's wedding in Italy we actually moved away from where Kirky was because he kept hammering on a negative note.

Gary Whetton should be regarded as a greater All Black than either Kirky or Buck, and as a captain he had almost everything, with just one significant exception.

He was a great player. Not a good player, a great player, fit to be in the top three All Blacks of his era. The best scrummager in his time, strong with good body position, and so fast he was certainly the best athlete in the tight five the All Blacks have had in the last 15 years. Over 100 metres he was one of the fastest guys in the whole team when he wound up. Robin Brooke is an athlete too, but he doesn't have the blazing speed that Gary had.

At training he was technically very, very good. Even with back play he knew what he wanted, and he loved the game of continuity, which a lot of tight forwards don't. Being so fast he loved the ball being moved around, and he shone out when it was.

On the field as captain his option taking was good. He didn't panic, just soaked up the pressure the way Buck did, and stayed calm, suggesting alternatives that might work.

When the decision was made to drop Buck in 1990, Gary was really the only logical choice as captain. I don't think any of the Auckland guys, including Gary, would have accepted me being captain, so Grizz Wyllie and the selectors, once they had decided Buck was out, made a sensible decision.

The biggest problem with Gary was a personality quirk that manifested itself in his arrogance to the younger players in the team, and sometimes his arrogance towards the public. I enjoyed Gary's company on and off the field personally, but sometimes I'd have to bite my tongue when he showed that other side to his nature. For that reason I never had the respect for him as captain that I had for Buck, or have now for Sean Fitzpatrick.

Gary's attitude seemed to be that the senior All Blacks were up on a pedestal, and everyone else was one or two steps below. When younger players came in he was very sarcastic to them, making a point of putting them in their place. That used to irk me, but I didn't confront him, because that would have caused a rift inside the team.

Really it was his only fault, but it caused problems. He didn't get the respect he should have got as a great player because of it. His attitude rubbed even Auckland players, like Craig Innes, up the wrong way. It didn't cause havoc, but it doesn't help if the captain pisses off some of the team.

Some of the problem may have been that when Gary was starting out Andy Haden was a major influence on him, and some of Andy's arrogance seemed to have rubbed off on Gary. By contrast Gary's twin brother, AJ, was a great buffer for Gary. AJ was very good with young players, and well liked by everyone. A natural clown, there were times when Gary would get himself into a difficult situation, and AJ would come in, make a joke, and clear the air.

It's not that unusual in sport to see the top performers finding it difficult to communicate with people they regard as not being in their league for skill and competitive temperament.

To my mind it's important that if there are players in a squad who are not up to the level of the very best players, and in a group of 15, or 21, or 30, there will always be varying degrees of ability, you certainly never make it known in front of the other players. That's like saying to someone who could be trying hard, "You're not up to it mate, bugger off."

The time to be totally honest about a player's ability is when you're in a selection meeting behind closed doors. That's when you have to say, "He's not ready for it," or "He hasn't got it."

I react best to a captain like Buck, who leads from the front, and shows great integrity in all his actions, on and off the field. The guidance he can give players, and the guidance he asks other players to give, is important too.

An All Black captain, even a provincial captain, needs to have a fair bit of knowledge of all positions in the game. If the captain is a forward he needs to have some understanding of the roles played by the second-five and the centre. In other words, if you want the game to flow, a forward leader needs a fair empathy with what your midfield backs are trying to achieve.

Motivationally, as a match gets near, a captain or coach is just topping off the preparation.

You won't have the time in the week leading up to a match to get round every player individually, but as you get to know the group you should be able to pick the collective mood.

If a team is well down, you need to start picking them up at the Tuesday night sessions before a Saturday game. Any later is too late. On the other hand, if they're on song there isn't any need to lift them up, in fact you might even run them a bit harder than they expected on Thursday, so they don't get up too soon.

A classic example in my experience of topping up a team was before Canterbury's Ranfurly Shield challenge with Waikato. Physically, Canterbury trained well, and all that was needed was for Vance Stewart and I to build up their confidence during the week, and to top it up on the Saturday. Vance did that very well, and the team responded with a winning, assured, performance.

By contrast, when Canterbury were due to play North Harbour in the semi-final of the '94 national provincial championship, we were flat from the aftermath of the Otago shield challenge at Lancaster Park. On the Tuesday we virtually flagged training, but on the Thursday, after five minutes it was obvious it was a waste of time. We tried to keep going, and train out the lethargy, but there was nothing there. We went to Auckland with the attitude it would either be a close game, or we'd lose by 40 points. We lost by 32.

So leadership, in my mind, is very much something that builds. It can't happen overnight, but is a process of knowledge. Knowing your players, your team, knowing what works, and what doesn't, and knowing how to put that knowledge into action.

13

To Win the Future

In business today, to stand still is to be left behind, to wither, and, eventually, to die.

And as we near the 21st century rugby in New Zealand must learn the lessons that have seen some economic giants of the 60s and 70s crash and burn, while more progressive corporates have prospered.

The secret is in change. The successful corporations have been unafraid of change, to the point where they embrace it. The New Zealand Rugby Union is not as resistant to change as they have been in the past, but they must act as quickly as possible, or be left behind in the race for people's leisure time, and the entertainment dollar.

It's not enough to keep doing what's worked in the past, no matter how successful that was. The time has come for rugby officials to be proactive and dynamic, to lead the game towards the year 2000.

There's no reason for them to be nervous about it. Rugby fans will accept changes to the game, sometimes easier than officials. As a good example, look at attitudes towards professionalism. Thirty years ago nobody thought it was ridiculous when travel firms could not advertise the names of retired All Blacks leading tour supporters' groups. Fifteen years ago Graham Mourie could be branded a professional for taking royalties from his autobiography. Today full professionalism would be totally accepted by 99 per cent of the population.

Early in 1995 an advertising expert made an excellent comparison between big, successful, well known brands, like the company I work for, Canterbury of New Zealand, and the All Blacks.

Big, extremely strong brands, he says, are like a steam train. Once you get the train up and running, you just need to keep it stoked regularly with coal, and it keeps roaring down the track.

But if you stop feeding it coal, it not only slows right down, but it also takes an enormous amount of energy to get it cranked up again.

It's exactly the same with rugby. If you lose the plot, and go down the wrong track, it takes a lot of time and effort, and you suffer a lot of criticism from outside parties, before you can get it cranked up and running efficiently again.

The New Zealand Rugby Union needs to look at its situation the way any other corporate would.

Basically the NZRFU is a manufacturer of a product, and it also markets that product. The NZRFU's main brand is "the All Blacks." The products are the players, and how they have them play the game.

You could make very close comparisons with Canterbury International Ltd. Our brand is Canterbury of New Zealand, and our products are the items of clothing that carry the brand.

There are no great secrets as to what's needed to ensure the longevity of your brand. You must invest time and resources.

At Canterbury if we stopped putting money into plant and machinery, into research, into design, then the brand would slow down.

It's vital that you find out what the end consumer of the process wants. The best manufactured and designed heavyweight jacket in the world will lose money if you only attempt to sell it in a tropical climate.

Rugby in New Zealand is starting to look more at what the consumer, the man or woman who buys tickets to the games – and gives the sport huge television audiences – wants.

Does the New Zealand rugby consumer want less lineouts, less mauling, less kicking? The NZRFU is only just getting into market research. Until now there's been a certain amount of guesswork as to what the consumers of rugby actually want.

We do know that probably the most burning issue facing the game now is professionalism. In New Zealand the demands on players begin in the first weekend of March, in the Super 10 series – soon to become Super 12 – and continue until December.

That sort of time commitment means there's no question that the sport is already professional, in that it largely denies players the chance to pursue and advance a career in anything other than rugby. Even if they're not being paid, players are training or playing for 12 months of the year.

I disagree with the argument that the New Zealand market is not big enough to fully fund eight or ten professional rugby provincial sides.

But to do so would need a change in the structure of rugby administration, provinces taking on responsibility for payment to players (with the help of funding from the NZRFU), while giving up some of their autonomy to the NZRFU, who would administer a draft system.

How would they all mesh together?

First, you could certainly run a provincial side on around $2 million a year. So you're looking at between $16 and $20 million for the whole country. If you ran two rounds of the national championship that sort of target is obtainable.

Obviously, to attract live, and television, audiences, and sponsors, the national competition must be competitive, with exciting, close games the norm, not the exception.

To achieve that a draft system for players would be essential. The draft is used extensively in all major professional sports in the United States, and it could work here, but only if there's a change in attitude towards who really runs the sport.

The NZRFU must be the central governing body of all New Zealand rugby, and, to a degree, provinces must give up some of their autonomy to the NZRFU.

Those in power rarely hand over control, but it can happen.

In Canterbury and Hawke's Bay, for example, the provincial rugby unions have recently streamlined their management methods, to allow the expertise of business people in the provinces to be used more profitably.

The draft would be administered by the NZRFU. Initially each coach would name his squad of, let's say, 17 players.

Every player not signed by a province would go into a pool. Any player not prepared to be available for the draft would not receive any of the central funding from the NZRFU.

First choice from the pool of players would go to the bottom placed team in the first division, then on up the standings. If the scouting and talent selection by the lower placed teams is good, then they'll start to make their way up the tables, and the competition would even out.

The selection from the draft pool could continue until each first division province had their original 17 players, plus five more to make up the squad of 22.

To my mind, the underlying objective is that anyone who is good enough to play provincial rugby at some level should not sit week after week as a reserve to an All Black.

In other words, if Auckland has two All Black locks, there's no point in an All Black Colt sitting on the reserve bench.

He'd be far better off to go to another union, even a second or third division side, where he might earn just as much money as he would have in Auckland.

If there was an allocation of funding from the NZRFU, a 19-year-old Colts player might be able to secure a good contract, go to the West Coast, and end up being their best player. Scouts from second and first division sides would see him. It could be that at the end of the season the Colt would be secured for the higher ranking side. The player dropped would go back into the draft.

It might not just be promising newcomers. In 1995 Southland would be the first team up to make a selection from the draft. Let's imagine Canterbury couldn't find room for an experienced player like Shayne Philpott. Southland, with a young backline, might go for his experience. Obviously it would also depend on where provinces perceived their own strengths and weaknesses.

With a draft system in place you should gradually move to a situation where instead of having three or four very strong teams in the national championship, you would have seven or eight.

As the competition became stronger it would certainly follow that revenue would increase, allowing fair payment to players.

The harsh reality for players in professional rugby though, would be that payments must be performance based, and some players will have a higher value than others. That will be a radical change from what's been regarded as a team sport in which everyone puts in a 100 per cent effort, and gets the same reward, basically victory, without any monetary compensation.

It's just a cruel fact that a spectacular, match winning winger like Jeff Wilson is likely to be worth more than a hard working, rarely sighted, prop forward.

And the provinces, not the NZRFU, would make the decisions on individual payments to players. That's how it works with the clubs in the Winfield Cup. The great bulk of players' salaries come from their clubs, so it's mainly prestige and honour that are the reasons for playing for Australia.

In the last two or three years some rugby players in New Zealand have started to use the All Blacks as a means to an end. They want to make the All Blacks to increase their market value when they head into an Australian league contract. So they aren't playing for the All Blacks for what most of us would feel are the right reasons.

If they could make their living from their province, contracted to Waikato or Counties rather than the All Blacks, then, in an odd twist, old fashioned pride would become by far the most important aspect of playing for the All Blacks. It would be the pinnacle of your rugby career, not an impressive page on your CV for a Sydney league club.

Marketing the game falls under four main headings, product and presentation, the laws, the media, and sponsorship.

PRODUCT AND PRESENTATION certainly covers the judiciary. Rugby really has to stand hard and fast here, and have some set rules.

No matter who is playing, or what game is coming up, if a player is caught performing an illegal act he's out for a certain length of time.

The biggest problem rugby has had in the past is that if someone is caught out, and there's a test coming up, he gets away with it. In the end that does you more damage than if you put the player out, and ran the risk of losing the test. You lose credibility with the public, the media, and sponsors.

We must look hard at venues, and when games are played. Are grounds more spartan than people want them to be in the 1990s? What entertainment do people want before and around a game? Would they prefer to go to rugby on a Friday night? On a Saturday or a Sunday?

Night rugby will emerge more strongly over the next few years, which means the very high costs of floodlighting must be faced. But that can be weighed against the fact that night games here are perfectly timed for breakfast viewing on northern hemisphere television.

Ticketing for major games should be closely examined, to make certain that regular customers, the most valued to rugby, get preferential bookings for the major games. Part of rugby's customer service must be to the continual brand user.

In other words, the people who go to see Fiji play New Zealand Maori or go to see early season provincial games, deserve some sort of points systems, so they're not shut out when the Bledisloe Cup test or the Springbok tour comes along.

In that area, individual unions must have some say in deciding what the market value of their product is. A blanket price for provincial games, even for tests, doesn't always make sense. A ticket to a test between New Zealand and Canada in Christchurch is not going to be worth a ticket to Otago's challenge for the Ranfurly Shield at Lancaster Park. There needs to be more flexibility in pricing.

LAWS really are a function of research and development. Research will tell you what spectators and players want from the game. Development needs to be encouraged, with new training techniques, so players don't get tired and bored.

Because of the way the world is moving, with electronic media and computers, in many fields anything that's been around for more than 18 months or two years is out of date.

Yet if you look at rugby, many coaches, and even players, still base their thinking on what they learned 10 years, or even longer, ago. It's a matter of really trying to keep up with the times.

MEDIA problems in New Zealand rugby largely revolve around the fact there's never been a consistent face for the game. The media feel there's often something being hidden, and internal arguments in rugby too often spill into the open.

Perhaps because the NZRFU hasn't been run like a professional corporate they haven't had the skills to discuss an approach with the media, and win respect and understanding for what they're trying to do.

It's a matter of tying it all up, and having what amounts to a Mr Rugby in New Zealand.

Ian Robson has done it superbly for league. Now, as soon as you mention the Auckland Warriors, you probably mention Ian Robson. The key is that Robson is the chief executive officer of the Warriors.

So whether it's marketing, sales, players, coaching, the lot, he has to have a handle on what's going on. Whether he has small or major knowledge, he has to have an idea. And that idea is expressed by one voice.

I don't believe appointing a media spokesperson, a public relations expert, is the answer. A media expert's role should only be in advising on ways and means.

But using a spokesperson who is not in a position of real power in the NZRFU is not good enough. Basically it has to be the chief executive officer, or someone of similar rank.

If you looked at the relationship between the media and the Warriors in the build-up to their start in the Winfield Cup there was a dramatic difference to the way the media treated rugby.

Largely because of how well Robson operated, the media knew there was always a story coming up. The media works with, but also against, the NZRFU. It's really a matter of having a relationship built up and built up. To do that it's essential that one person is in the driving seat. Too many spokespeople just clouds the issue, and leads to damage control, rather than initiating good publicity.

It's a matter of training, of looking at relations between the players and the media, administrators and the media, provincial unions and the NZRFU, to ensure there are no conflicts being conducted through the media, and how well the judiciary process is understood by the media, and, by extension, the public.

SPONSORSHIP will always be around in sport, because it is so easy to tie brands in with hero worship. In some cases, for a business, it's a far cheaper medium to use than direct advertising.

What finally counts in sponsorship is that the positioning of the brand and the sport make the right fit. Sponsors have to look at how closely they can align themselves with the product. Then, to be blunt, they have to see if the sponsorship drives sales.

A sponsor must know where a sport is going, and in a new style, dynamic, national competition, with more even teams, and two rounds, there would be more scope for the NZRFU to go to the major corporates for naming rights to provincial teams.

Why not Fletcher Auckland, Brierleys Wellington, maybe Lane Walker Rudkin Canterbury or Comalco Otago? That's where the best possible relationship with the media becomes so important, to overcome what might be initial resistance to "branded" teams. A good, fair environment that works for the sponsors will drive the competition, which ultimately is good for everyone, including the media.

The fit of brand with team and sport is important. For instance, if you look at the fit between Canterbury of New Zealand and the All Blacks, it's pretty much ideal. Like Steinlager, another major sponsor, we're a premium brand, and the All Blacks are probably New Zealand's premium sporting brand.

The Warriors are aiming to broaden their base of support by targeting white collar workers. Traditionally in this country league has been a blue collar sport. It's a very clever marketing strategy, because they know they'll retain their historic base, they just want to add a higher socio economic group as well. Their sponsorship is not quite as nice a fit as Steinlager is with the All

Blacks though, because DB Bitter is a mass market brand, and the Warriors are looking for their growth further upmarket.

Looking at the broad picture, rugby is fighting for the entertainment dollar, with league, with horse racing, with movies, with computer games, with any number of other sports and diversions that weren't a factor even 10 years ago.

To recap, it's my belief that rugby can maintain a winning edge by:-

* Changing the administrative structure, so more changes are driven from the NZRFU

* Having provinces agree to the NZRFU having the same degree of control over provinces that the New South Wales Rugby League does over Winfield Cup clubs

* Introducing a two round national provincial championship

* Introducing professionalism to provincial rugby

* With the help of central funding, having the players contracted to their unions, who would provide the bulk of a player's income

* Levelling the playing field by having a draft system for provincial rugby, controlled by the NZRFU

* Restoring the mana of playing for the All Blacks, by making it an honour, not a means, to make a living

* Researching what consumers want from rugby, not assuming officials know what is good for the public

* If necessary, changing laws in response to consumer demand

* Tightening up on judicial systems

* Making sure regular supporters get preferential treatment for tickets for big games

* Producing a "Mr Rugby" who can speak with authority for the NZRFU to the media and the public

* Fitting major sponsors with provincial teams

The task facing rugby in this country is a big one. We can't put our heads in the sand, and assume that rugby will automatically command the major audience. Ultimately, in the race for the winning edge, the sport that best looks after the needs of the consumer is the one that will succeed.

14

No Safety Nets

I have never seen discussions inside a team as brutally honest as on the very first day of the All Black build-up to the 1995 World Cup.

We'd all travelled to Queenstown, a training squad of 30 players, with wives and partners, for an exercise designed to build spirit more than fitness, understanding more than muscle.

During the camp several of the players bungy jumped, flying off a bridge with nothing between themselves and the rocks and water below than a thick rubber cord tied round their ankles.

But inside our resort hotel, in private group sessions, we were free falling without a safety net or restraining line.

Laurie Mains invited us to very open and frank about what we saw as the problems that had to be overcome to win the World Cup.

It was quickly agreed that in '93 and '94 we hadn't been fit or strong enough, whereas we had been fit in '92.

From there the analysis would usually be personal. You'd look at your own fitness and commitment levels, decide what you needed to do to get better.

But this was different. In the past you might think that somebody else wasn't physical enough in the lineouts, or that his communication was poor, or that he was a bad tackler on one side, or that he didn't push hard enough in the scrums.

You'd think it, but you wouldn't say it. This time we did. It was dangerous, potentially a disaster, but instead of flaring up, everyone took it right on the chin, and you could feel the whole squad just close together like a fist.

What was even more incredible was that the guns then turned on Laurie and his selection panel, and they copped a fullscale assault on their tactics, the selection process where they tried to change players' positions, and players being selected and not given a chance to cement their places in the team.

On the issue of tactics young players like Josh Kronfeld questioned the idea of using runners one off the ruck to get in behind the opposition. "That's the safest option," he said, "but it's not the only one."

Eventually a collective agreement was forged over the style of play we wanted to take into the Cup. We pledged to be fitter than any other team in South Africa, and to move the ball until the opposition was spread, then throw someone into a hole.

That was on the first day. On the second day Laurie said it was exactly what they wanted, real honesty, that knocked the ego out of players, and helped create an environment where players want to do it for each other, not for themselves.

If you look back to '87 that was very much a team effort, but in '91 there was a big bunch of egos bouncing off each other.

Several personality conflicts were cleared away in Queenstown. I'd had some personal conflict with Craig Dowd, the Auckland prop. In my view some of his behaviour wasn't acceptable for an All Black. It seemed to me that at times there was a lack of respect for senior players, which by extension is a lack of respect for the tradition of the All Blacks, and that sometimes, with a few beers on board, his discipline slips with the public.

Now he probably thought that I was a boring old bastard, and that as an All Black he could make his own mind up on what was right and wrong. But we thrashed it out, and by the end of the weekend things were fine.

Throughout the team we cleared the air, started from scratch, and created an environment where team spirit could grow. On tour, in some ways, it's harder to get a good feeling among the players, because in the individual positions you're competing with each other.

But in camp, especially at the early ones, we weren't competing, so a more supportive culture develops, where even if the guy is in the same position as you, you want him to be doing his best, because the team, or the results the team can gain, supercede your own ego.

It was a pity in Queenstown that into this developing atmosphere was dropped a great sponsorship idea, but a potential bombshell with team building - the black Fords. At the end of the World Cup the limited edition Falcons would be auctioned, with proceeds going to the All Black Club. That was a big sponsorship boost, but the trick was that squad members would get to use them up to the Cup, and they were about 10 cars short of covering the whole squad.

The announcement of who would actually get the cars was made by Laurie, and it was like a test side being read out.

First he explained that the main criteria was geographical. You could almost hear the hearts sinking among the Auckland and North Harbour players. At the time only Richard Loe and I were in the squad from Canterbury (Andrew Mehrtens and Graeme Bachop were added later). A company car could disqualify you. My heart sunk at that. But that could be outweighed by seniority. In the end Richard and I were both on the list, and we certainly enjoyed the use of what were really luxury cars.

Ultimately they would not be a divisive factor inside the team, but if anything similar was to happen in the future, I'd suggest it should either be one for all, or none at all. There was a public statement by Alama Ieremia over him not getting a car in Wellington, while Earle Kirton did, and there was certainly potential for rifts to be created over the cars.

Our next camp was in Auckland, in December, and we went through more sessions that involved a lot of talking. I spoke with Laurie in Auckland, saying I thought we had wasted a chance to do the sort of work we would need to play the game of continuity in Africa.

He said he wanted to let the players have some recovery time from the previous season, and let me know, through a third person, that I should reserve judgement until after the February camp in Taupo.

And there he certainly made up for any lack of physical activity in Auckland. The four days of training were the hardest I've ever had in my life. I've had some hard training with Laurie over the years, but this was the toughest.

The intensity didn't ease up. We'd go from the scrum machine to the tackle bags to 120 metre runs to working in mini-units on skills, then taking them into a team situation. For the forwards especially the work demanded was incredible.

We'd end the day with 150 metre stride outs, then down and ups, and start the next morning with a 3km time trial. That rolled on into more bag work, more 150s, in two big sessions every day. People who were there as spectators were staggered by what we were doing.

You were too scared to eat at lunchtime, because you weren't exactly sure what you were going to get in the afternoon. You couldn't take too much on board, but you did need to have enough energy to get you through the afternoon session, with hopefully enough left over to walk onto the bus, and get back to the hotel and into a spa pool, so you'd be able to do it again the next day.

We didn't get a huge amount of sleep either. We went out on a boat on the lake a couple of nights, getting home at about 11 or midnight, and we wanted to be up early enough to have a proper breakfast before you started training again.

In retrospect the intensity of the training helped bind the team together even more. Shared discomfort is a great unifier, and the guys that struggled really got encouragement to get through.

In the fitness tests at Taupo I was impressed, as I have been many times over the years, with Ian Jones, and his ability, for such a tall, rangy guy to move so quickly in the beep tests. The beep test is pretty basic. Lines of cones are set up, 20 metres apart. You run from one line to the other, in a reasonable amount of time. Then the time gets reduced by a second each sprint, and you have to run the 20 metres before a machine beeps. Ian can turn and get up to speed in a remarkably short time.

Jon Preston and Graeme Bachop are always very fit, but the ones who impressed me the most were the big tight forwards; Craig Dowd, Fitzy, Mark Allen, Richard Loe and Robin Brooke were very, very fit.

It was a good start, but in the past coaches and management had set levels of fitness that guys were supposed to achieve, and if the levels weren't met the players were supposed to get the flick. But that never really occurred.

This was the first year it did happen. Ultimatums were put on Jonah Lomu, Mark Cooksley and Waisake Sotutu who were excluded from the camps until they got up to the levels. They got three weeks to meet the requirements, and Waisake and Mark didn't make it, so they were excluded. That sent a message to the other players that they were serious about fitness targets being met.

By the time we got to the test against Canada, and the final trial in Whangarei, we were fitter as a group than we had been in 1992.

When you're fit enough to know that you can push as hard as you want to, there's no need to hold back during a game to get through it. Our confidence started to grow in Taupo, when we got through the weekend, and then, with monthly testing, we saw our results getting better and better.

That leads to a team having a lot more confidence as a group, because individually you start to back your own aerobic fitness and strength. Even more importantly there was virtually no ego in the group when we left for Africa.

It was a level playing field for everyone. Younger players like Andrew Mehrtens and Simon Culhane came into a situation where there wasn't a pecking order that looked down on newcomers.

So Mehrts could come into the test team against Canada, show his skills to a degree where he was named player of the day, and not have anybody in the squad looking sideways at him as some sort of new star on the block. The old school didn't get dirty about it.

There was a slight air of uncertainty going into the Canadian test, our one international before we played at the World Cup. BJ Lochore had suggested publicly that it was a very important game for the All Blacks, not only for our own confidence, but also to cement public support for the team.

Canada had a poor provincial record going into the test, but so did Ireland in 1992, and they gave the All Blacks a real battle in the first test, almost rolling them. Like Ireland in '92, the Canadians played a spoiling sort of game, which could have brought them rewards if we'd been inaccurate and made errors.

We did turn over a bit of ball early on, but we weren't punished for it, and once we got a real hold on the game we managed to concentrate for almost the whole of the match. It is very easy, once you're well ahead, to go off the boil, but we kept our focus pretty well.

Eventually we were pretty satisfied, not just for the fact we won 73-7, but because we were able to put into play the moves we'd been working on in training.

We saw Andrew Mehrtens set a world record for points on debut (28) and Graeme Bachop playing with the freedom that he brings to his game when he is relaxed and enjoying his rugby. Grim says that in his early test days he thought more about not making mistakes than anything else. Obviously enjoying life in Japan, he returned to New Zealand to prepare for the World Cup with a spring in his step, and it was reflected in the way he played.

Unlike England, who went to the World Cup after amazing scenes between captain Will Carling and their officials (in Will's words "the old farts") we felt fine about the men in charge of the 1995 campaign.

As time went by it was obvious that our management team was very well balanced. Earle Kirton was a very good buffer for Laurie. When Laurie gets uptight, Earle will chuck in a one liner that can ease the tension quite a lot.

The players have limitless respect for Colin Meads and BJ Lochore. They're All Black greats, and they pass on a lot of knowledge and experience to the guys, and the players really feed off it. BJ is very articulate when it comes to dealing with the media, the public and the players. Pinetree would be the first to say that if he and BJ want to say the same thing, it will somehow sound better coming from BJ. So they make a very good pairing. Some of the aspects of the management side that Pinetree doesn't like, BJ will pick up, so the relationship works very smoothly.

Colin never felt threatened by the possibility of BJ in effect taking over his managerial position, and BJ's never likely to even consider doing it. Their natures, and the way they are, is that by just being themselves, they can work together perfectly.

In Whangarei, after the final trial, the players were able to go to a room by themselves to hear the squad named. It gave those who made it the chance to pass on condolences to the guys who missed out. The hard part about a team announcement is that there's never much jubilation because you feel so much for the players who have missed out.

The vast majority of the squad had been tipped by rugby journalists quizzed in *Rugby News* magazine during the week, but no matter how sure the media might be that you'll make it, hearing your name actually read out is a good feeling.

Two who came through late in the day were Ant Strachan and Paul Henderson. At the end of '94 Ginge had been contemplating retirement, but with Southland making the first division he decided to hold on for another year.

After a good tour of Canada and the Pacific Islands with the Divisional team, he was given a chance in the North-South match, and grabbed it. His loyalty to his home province paid off for him, and I was delighted. He was playing as well as he ever had, and you know with Ginge that he'll never have a bad game. The bigger the occasion, the stronger he plays.

Ant must have been a close call at halfback with Stu Forster. They're both chirpy, lively, characters, and in the end it must have very much come down to Ant's trial form. When he's on his game his kicking is very good.

There was certainly a feeling that we were playing some good rugby, and we'd go to South African with our own high expectations of what we could achieve.

15

Blazing Away

On our last day in Johannesburg, the Tuesday after the 1995 World Cup final, I presented a small gift to Sean Fitzpatrick, on behalf of the team.

I said that it was a great reflection on Sean, on his captaincy, and the way he is as an individual, that we had been an All Black team without internal divisions. Sean says it was actually the happiest All Black team he's ever been involved in, which includes every side since 1986.

Sean takes a lot of pride in his own play, but within the team, and externally to the public and the media and the rugby fraternity, he doesn't have a huge ego, as some of the frontline players have in the past. If you have a lot of senior players who are egotistical, then that frame of mind quickly turns to arrogance.

At the World Cup, by his example, along with Laurie Mains, Colin Meads and Brian Lochore, who all think the same way, Sean made it a level playing field for everybody, and that attitude sunk deep into the fabric of the team.

It was reflected in many ways. For example, if things hadn't gone well at a training session some of the players, often the younger ones, would say, "Right, let's all be up for breakfast together at 7.30 tomorrow, so we can talk about training, and get things rolling." In the past guys would sort of dribble in to breakfast, then try to get things to jell on the training ground.

The togetherness meant that we never had, as some of the British media tried to suggest, any jealousy when interest in Jonah Lomu started to reach a fever pitch.

It was very simple to the rest of the team. If 14 of us could put Jonah into a position where he could use his talents to beat a man, score a try, or set someone else up for a try, then we were delighted. After all, isn't that what rugby is supposed to be all about?

We arrived in South Africa 11 days before our opening game of the Cup, against Ireland, and at first we were just getting our lungs used to the thin air high on the veldt.

There was a bit of a run in Johannesburg, nothing like the killers we'd been having in New Zealand, and then we travelled 145km to Sun City, a hotel/entertainment complex that's like a little Las Vegas set in the middle of nowhere.

There's an artificial surf beach, a casino, exotic hotels modelled on ancient ruins, and it was a great place to relax. There was no gap later in the tournament to do so.

The fun was soon knocked on the head when we returned to Johannesburg. At altitude you start to breathe heavily, and your throat becomes dry just from the warm-up jogging. Laurie ran us hard at the Police College, and guys like myself, Zinny Brooke and Olo Brown, who suffer from minor asthma problems, were using our Ventalin inhalers frequently. Sean suffered a blood nose. We knew the real work had begun.

But the first pool game, against Ireland, seemed to take forever to arrive. We'd all put so much time and effort into the World Cup that we were very nervous before the game. It was a night game too, and we made the mistake of watching two other matches on TV before we played. You get involved in the matches you watch, and you're mentally a wee bit drained when you play yourself. We didn't do that again.

While we knew we could beat Ireland, we also knew they'd get in amongst us, and play a very physical game. And they certainly did. While Jonah marked his potential with some big runs, most of us were unhappy with the way things went, although we did win, 43-19.

After the game there was a real honesty session, and with the matches coming thick and fast after the opener, some of us were grateful that we were selected for the next match, against Wales.

Before the Welsh test their Australian coach, Alec Evans, had suggested that the weak link in the All Blacks was in the forwards. We all saw the quotes, and went out determined to blitz them up front, and give our backs good enough ball to run with.

It was probably the only game in the Cup where we reverted to fairly patterned, old style, All Black rugby. We kept it tight and took them on in the forwards, where at times we should have run the ball. In the wake of Alec's remarks we did want to see how good they were. In the end it was a 34-9 victory, so the win was quite comprehensive.

Having said that, we were still not right back to where we had been at the trials, or even the North-South game in New Zealand. We discovered at the Cup that almost every side there was good enough to score if you made a mistake.

That surprised us a little, but we saw it happen again and again. Sides like Italy and Argentina gave the top seeds in their pools tough games. One of the good things about the '95 World Cup was that most teams did not come to South Africa to contain, which is what often happens when playing against stronger countries. Most sides wanted to attack.

Even the Japanese, on the wrong side of a world record 145-17 loss at Bloemfontein, seized on what were probably the only three mistakes the All Blacks made all afternoon and scored two tries and a penalty from them. It showed the preparation that every side in South Africa had put in. They were all good enough to take every opportunity even the best sides offered them, and to take points from them.

There was always the potential for the Japanese game to be a high scoring one, but just how high the score gets in games like that is determined by how well the stronger team prepares. The greater the effort at training the more likely the score will creep to 60, 80 or 100 points.

It was a chance for the All Black management to give every guy in the squad a game, and the scoreline showed the effort they put into it. It's a bit sad to see a team at the World Cup having 145 points scored against it, but it was a reflection of the healthy competition in almost every position in our squad.

In the front row the props were even, and among the loose forwards Josh Kronfeld was the only one to sew up his position early on, because he was playing so well. Even there Paul Henderson had an excellent game as captain against Japan. There was certainly pressure among the rest of the loose forwards, with Blair Larsen probably looking at playing from the quarter-final onwards if he hadn't been injured in the Japanese game.

There was no gap in this team between the haves and the have nots. Every player was equal until the call had to be made on the playing 15 for the tests. With selection came the responsibility to go out and perform for the whole team.

The quarter-final with Scotland was the start of the knockout phase. The Big Five, as they were called, South Africa, Australia, England, France and the All Blacks, were all still in contention, although the Australians had looked suspect losing the opening game of the tournament to the Springboks.

After we'd beaten Scotland 48-30 in Pretoria there were suggestions that we might have looked vulnerable late in the game, when they ran in a couple of tries.

It certainly had nothing to do with a lack of physical fitness. This was the fittest All Black team I've ever played in. It was really just human nature.

While you're on the field you're not thinking, "We've got a tough game coming up next weekend in the semi-final." But when the game is in the bag, you remember it's a quarter-final, not the only game that everyone wants to win at a World Cup, the final. So, rather like a motor racing driver, if you're a minute in front you don't hammer the car.

If it was a three test series it would be different. Even if you were 2-0 up in the series, and leading by 30 points in the last test, you'd want to drill it home that you were the dominant side. But nobody will really remember the game with Scotland when they look back on the Cup. So you do ease up psychologically.

Beating Scotland put us into a semi-final against England, who had beaten the Wallabies, 25-22. The other semi-final set France against South Africa. France had beaten Ireland 36-12, while South Africa had lowered Western Samoa 42-14 in a fierce game that left players on both sides nursing injuries.

Of all the teams at the 1995 World Cup this All Black side wanted to beat England more than any other. After the loss in 1993 at Twickenham, when the English players had been gloating about their win, a similar sort of mood built up to how the All Blacks felt in 1990 before the test in Nantes.

In 1990 enough of us had been in the 1986 side (who had lost to a ferocious French team) to desperately want to avenge the defeat. In '90 we played with pace and intensity, and really blew the French off the field.

Those sort of games only come round once or twice in a 10 year career, and before the English game in Cape Town, down at sea level, Sean, Richard Loe, Zinny (with whom I roomed) and I talked about wanting to blitz England at the start.

That was exactly what happened. For the first time in the tournament we exploited what we believed was our superior fitness. We wanted to move the English around. They like going from set piece to set piece, which suits their big forwards.

To really benefit from our aerobic fitness we needed to reduce errors, and keep control of the ball. It was important that we matched them in the set pieces though, because if we didn't they could fan out, and knock us over in the midfield.

So in the week leading into the semi-final we sweated on scrums and lineouts, more than at any previous stage. But while we were working on the set pieces we also wanted to set our targets wide.

That started with the kickoff, when Andrew Mehrtens switched the direction of the attack, and Jonah ended up scoring a remarkable try, which he completed by running over the top of the English fullback.

After 11 minutes we were leading 15-0. At halftime it was 25-3, and two minutes into the second half it was 30-3. We could see it in the eyes of the English players, by scoring like that against them, they were shell shocked.

We took the chance to test out what is usually one of England's strengths, their defensive screen from a set piece.

I'd looked at a video of their defence from a scrum on the left hand blind. Basically, Dean Richards, their No. 8, lined out, then Rob Andrew, then the wing. I said to Laurie that I'd like to try a move to hold Dean Richards. We called it an eight (Zinny) to nine (Graeme) with the flanker as a dummy cutting in. We didn't ever run it in training, but we did walk it through.

The first time we had the chance to use it, Zinny and I had a brief dispute over the call. He said, "We'll do Bongo." I said, "No, this is the one we'll score from, the Black-Two-Flash." In the end we pulled the Black-Two-Flash. It worked like a charm, and I couldn't help but applaud as Grim (Bachop) ran the try in.

I honestly think that England are going to have to change their game plan if they want to win the World Cup, or beat southern hemisphere countries in a test series.

They play a kicking game, trying to force the opposition into errors so they can kick goals to win. As the game gets more and more professional it has to become more aesthetically pleasing to the public and to the television companies. A Rupert Murdoch is not going to pay big broadcasting fees to see a team win 12-9, four kicks to three.

Before we beat England, the Springboks had beaten the French in Durban, where it never rains in the winter. This time it rained so much the match was delayed for 90 minutes, and so the final all South Africa, from President Mandela down, had wanted so badly was on.

On the Thursday night before the Saturday final at Ellis Park gastric illness swept through the All Black squad. In a later head count we found that 22 out of the official party of 35 had suffered, and 10 out of the 15 players in the final had been ill at some stage before kickoff.

We'll never know what the cause was. There were some who believed it was food poisoning, some who thought it was a viral problem. Zinny and I, who roomed together, escaped without any ill effects. If it was viral then we might have been spared because we wanted a quiet room.

The first room we were allocated was right beside the lift. So we asked if we could be moved, and we went to the other end of a long wing. By accident we were a little bit isolated from the rest of the side. I'd also been slightly unwell early in the trip, so if it was viral I may have built up some immunity.

It certainly wasn't an excuse for our loss in the final, but it would be untrue to say it didn't take some of our focus away leading into the game. On the Friday, when we went for the last time to Ellis Park before the final, Goldie (Jeff Wilson) was too sick to come on the bus with us. So instead of only thinking about the game we were wondering about what was causing the illnesses, and who was sick and who wasn't.

We were in the changing shed when the South African Airways 747 flew low over the ground, but you could tell just from walking onto the ground before the match that it was a special day. I love going out and soaking up the atmosphere before a game, looking at our supporters, looking at the opposition's. It looked as if every Springbok fan in the crowd had a South African flag. I have never seen so many flags at a test match. It all helps you get hyped up for the game.

Very little of the match had gone before we found the South Africans had really done some work on countering our backline. In the end that would be the winning of the match for them.

Where most backlines play an inside-out defence, they played an outside-in defence, looking at pincering Jonah so he couldn't beat his man, James Small, on the outside. They put Small on his outside, and with their centre moving on him from the inside they shut him down really well.

To a certain extent the occasion might have got to us as a team. We'd been playing a style of running rugby, and in the first half we were moving the ball laterally across the field. We should perhaps have been putting the ball in behind them a bit to put the pressure on them.

There were certainly comparisons that could be made with Otago's 1994 challenge against Canterbury for the Ranfurly Shield. At Ellis Park we were almost trying to play catch-up rugby when we were only three points behind, and because they'd done so much work on their defensive screen they were knocking us over when we kept chancing our arm.

Then, in the second half, when we were actually getting better ball, we'd just lost a wee bit of confidence to start moving it around. When we all look at the video down the track we'll learn from what happened. But it was all part of the occasion.

Certainly there was really nothing between the two teams. After 104 minutes of rugby it came down to three points, and we had the chance to win it three minutes from the end. Mehrts was unlucky enough to not hit the dropped goal.

I said to him afterwards, and really meant every word, "Don't ever think that it was you who lost it."

We came to the World Cup determined to attack, and to score tries. If you score tries, then nobody can say you didn't deserve to win. The final of the World Cup was the only game in which we didn't score a try, so for the first time it just came down to kicks. They got one more than we did.

It was hugely frustrating, and totally demoralising, but that's the harsh reality of sport.

My final came to an end at halftime, but the trouble had actually begun at the Thursday training run at Sandton College. In the last minutes of training I spun on my knee, and I felt the cartilage tear.

The next day, at Ellis Park, the All Black doctor, Mike Bowen, injected some long lasting anaesthetic into the back of my knee. I had a jog around, and it was fine. So when it came to the game he hit me again. This time he hit a nerve. Early in the game I felt my foot starting to roll over. When we called a short kickoff I went to jump and it just went out on me. It wasn't a twisted ankle in the game, as it probably looked, it was the same nightmare of a foot going to sleep that happened in the Queensland game back in '88. I watched the second half and the extra time from the reserves bench on the sideline.

The official dinner after the final would prove to be a lot more newsworthy than the usual starchy, formal show.

Dr Louis Luyt, the president of the South African Rugby Union, was not due to speak, but he took the stage anyway, dragging up his son-in-law, the tournament director, Rian Oberholzer. The content of Luyt's speech went from bad to worse.

He really got on a roll when he talked about South Africa not being invited to the '87 and '91 World Cups. The result at Ellis Park proved, he said, that if they'd been there they would have won those as well. At first there was a stunned silence in the hall, then people started chipping him.

Then he invited Derek Bevan, the Welsh referee who had controlled the game's South Africa had won against Australia and France, to the stage to accept a gold watch. Somebody at our table muttered, "At least in the past they tried to hide it."

Sir Ewart Bell, the chairman of the Rugby World Cup, then spoke, and when he'd finished I said to Colin Meads, our All Black manager, who I was sitting next to, "Tree, can I go and have a word with Louis?" Colin said, "Yeah, feel free."

I was determined I would not raise my voice, or swear at all. I introduced myself very politely, said I was a member of the All Black party, and thanked him for the tournament.

Then I said, "I'd just like you to do one thing for me, Dr Luyt. Get hold of the video of tonight's function, including your speech, and go through the content. Because 95 per cent of the people in this hall are astounded with the way in which you've presented yourself, and what you've said."

He went straight on the attack. He shouted at me and said I was a typical New Zealander, who couldn't take losing, that I was a pig. He started swearing at me.

I told him that I would not raise my voice, or swear at him, which only made him get worse. I didn't find it hard to keep control, because I didn't want my point to be lost in a shouting match. He really showed his true colours.

Eventually I said, "Look, Louis, nobody is ever bigger than the game itself, although you like to think you are. You've upset what should have been a fantastic day for South African rugby, the country, and world rugby."

At that stage Richie Guy, the chairman of the New Zealand Rugby Union, came in and said, "I think he's got the message."

The French and Australian rugby presidents were there too. They certainly hadn't disagreed with what I'd been saying.

I went and had a chat with John Sturgeon, a former All Black manager, who said, "Well, at least somebody's told him what we think." Later we heard that Paul Henderson had gone to Luyt, introduced himself, and said he wanted to congratulate South Africa on a fine win, which they deserved. As Luyt went to shake hands Paul said, "But as far as you're concerned, personally, you're just a big fat zero." Paul circled his finger and thumb in case Luyt had misunderstood what he meant.

What Louis Luyt might never see, but I think most New Zealanders did, was that this was an All Black team who brought back to world rugby an open, running style.

Teams coached by Alan Jones, and then Bob Dwyer in Australia, kicked the ball long, and had a very organised defensive screen that knocked the opposition over. It's a myth that the Wallabies played a truly expansive game when they won the World Cup in '91.

The one person I felt really happy for at the '95 Cup was Laurie Mains. He took some terrible stick over the previous three years, but he had the courage to allow the players to be deeply involved in determining the style of rugby we would play.

At that Queenstown camp back in October of '94 it was Jeff Wilson who started it all rolling by standing up and saying, "Why do you, Laurie, and the senior players decide on the game plan? Why can't we all decide?"

For me that was where the whole thing turned. The players became accountable because they had input into the game plan, and Laurie determined the fitness levels and tuned the tactics to meet the players' needs.

That was the first time, in my experience of Laurie, that he didn't determine the type of players he wanted, and the game he wants them to play. By giving the players the choice we arrived at an unpredictable game. Only South Africa managed to contain it.

And some of the younger players will be tempered by the reverse at Ellis Park. I saw it happen with Jeff Wilson after the loss to England in '93. Goldie took that hard, but even before the World Cup I thought he'd grown immensely as a man since '93, and I see him being one of the players taking the backs through to the next World Cup.

I agree with Brian Lochore, who feels that Andrew Mehrtens will be a bit harder mentally and personally after the World Cup. Like several of the younger guys Mehrts had a bit of a dream run into the team. A couple of times during the Cup I had a go at him about being a little late for team meetings.

Like any very good first-five he took missing the dropped goal near the end of time personally. He'll be a stronger character for the experience, as upsetting as it was for him, but I hope he never loses his character and jovial personality. That's the way Mehrts is, and that's the way he operates best.

Josh Kronfeld is a dedicated footballer, who takes a lot of pride in his performance, and works hard to maintain it. He was Johnny on the spot through the Cup, which certainly suited the wide ranging style of play.

However, my players of the tournament are the All Black tight-five. They were the ones who really allowed the All Blacks to get the ball wide. Without their aerobic fitness we wouldn't have had them crashing into rucks and turning the ball over. They were the rock on which our whole game was based.

The star of the tournament, of course, was Jonah. After being dropped after the French tests in '94, and then struggling with his fitness at the training camps over summer he obviously went away, and sought a lot of advice from people he trusts and believes in.

When the team assembled to play as the Harlequins in Hamilton at Easter he was full of fire. When they trained he was like a runaway steam train. He didn't just impress the management, but the other players as well.

He's an intelligent man to sense that by putting the effort in he was making an immense impression on the players. In that atmosphere he went from strength to strength. The background work he'd done improved his defensive game, turning, going back, taking high kicks.

On attack he just did what came naturally, and now I'd say there's not a sports follower in the world who doesn't know who Jonah Lomu is.

Amongst the older All Blacks it was going out and giving it 100 per cent at every training run, busting his butt for the team, that earned Jonah the respect he now has. That was the way the old school brought us up, and though things have changed, and there isn't the heirachal system there used to be, there's still that respect that has to be earned.

I hope that's never lost. To me it's the key element in the All Blacks' success over the years. Without it we're just another rugby team.

I leave the game as rugby is drastically changing. Hopefully the changes in 1996 will allow New Zealand to keep the outstanding younger players, even someone as keenly sought by league as Jonah.

We're perhaps a little thin on the ground for halfbacks, and for locks, but there's no reason why the style of game we started at the '95 World Cup, and some of the outstanding, and still young, men who played it can't put All Black rugby right back on top for the next three to four years.

MICHAEL R BREWER

FIRST CLASS CAREER RECORD TO JUNE 30, 1995

	Year	Played	Won	Lost	Drew	No 8	Flanker	Tries
Otago	1985	15	9	5	1	11	4	6
	1986	12	7	5	-	11	1	3
	1987	12	8	4	-	1	11	2
	1988	15	11	3	1	-	15	3
	1989	10	7	3	-	-	10	6
	1990	10	6	4	-	-	10	3
	1991	7	6	1	-	1	6	2
	1992	12	9	3	-	1	11	1
		93	**63**	**28**	**2**	**25**	**68**	**26**
Canterbury	1993	3	2	1	-	-	3	-
	1994	11	8	3	-	1	10	3
	1995	2	-	2	-	-	2	-
		16	**10**	**6**	**-**	**1**	**15**	**3**
New Zealand	1986	9	6	3	-	6	3	2
	1987	5	5	-	-	-	5	4
	1988	8	8	-	-	-	8	2
	1989	9	9	-	-	-	9	3
	1990	10	8	2	-	3	7	-
	1991	2	2	-	-	2	-	-
	1992	4	3	1	-	-	4	1
	1993	1	1	-	-	-	1	-
	1994	6	2	3	1	-	6	-
	1995	5	4	1	-	2	3	-
		59	**48**	**10**	**1**	**13**	**46**	**12**
Trials	1986	1	1	-	-	-	1	-
	1987	1	1	-	-	1	-	1
	1988	1	-	1	-	-	1	-
	1989	1	-	1	-	-	1	-
	1992	1	-	1	-	-	1	-
	1994	2	2	-	-	-	2	-
	1995	1	-	1	-	-	1	-
NZ Colts	1985	4	4	-	-	2	2	-
NZ Uni	1984	1	1	-	-	1	-	-
	1985	8	8	-	-	2	6	2
SI Uni	1984	1	-	1	-	-	1	-
South Island	1986	1	-	1	-	1	-	-
	1995	1	-	1	-	1	-	-
South Zone	1987	1	-	1	-	1	-	-
	1988	2	1	1	-	-	2	-
Barbarians	1986	1	-	1	-	1	-	-
	1987	4	4	-	-	1	3	4
Sassenachs	1986	1	1	-	-	1	-	-
		33	**23**	**10**	**-**	**12**	**21**	**7**
TOTALS		**201**	**144**	**54**	**3**	**51**	**150**	**48**